# COOKING FOR CHRISTMAS

Cover Photo: Medley of Christmas foods

# COOKING FOR CHRISTMAS

**Rosemary Wadey**

# CONTENTS

**ANOTHER BEST-SELLING VOLUME FROM HPBooks®**
**Publisher:** Rick Bailey; **Editorial Director:** Elaine R. Woodard; **Editor:** Jeanette P. Egan
**Art Director:** Don Burton; **Book Assembly:** Leslie Sinclair
**Typography:** Cindy Coatsworth, Michelle Carter; **Director of Manufacturing:** Anthony B. Narducci
**Recipe testing by International Cookbook Services:** Barbara Bloch, President; Rita Barrett, Director of Testing; Nancy Strada, Tester

**Published by HPBooks, Inc.**
P.O. Box 5367, Tucson, AZ 85703      602/888-2150
ISBN 0-89586-348-0
Library of Congress Catalog Card Number 85-68378
© 1985 HPBooks, Inc.      Printed in the U.S.A.
1st Printing

Originally published as Cooking for Christmas ©1984 Hennerwood Publications Limited

However it is celebrated, Christmas is always a time of gaiety and celebration. It is also a time when special foods are prepared and served. Every family has certain foods that are a part of its Christmas tradition. It just wouldn't be Christmas without them. Other families like to explore new ideas for holidays and start new traditions.

This book covers every aspect of holiday food, from the most traditional Christmas dinner to simple suppers and cocktail parties. There are suggested menus for special meals during the holidays. This will provide new ideas, and perhaps, create some new family favorites. Whatever your preference, this book was written to make entertaining easier during the Christmas season. Start your planning early with the aid of the menus and the foods that can be made ahead.

## COOKING AHEAD

The simplest way to reduce the problem of having too much to do in too little time is to cook ahead. This is even easier if you have a freezer. The well-prepared cook with a carefully planned calendar of events has a tremendous advantage over those who leave planning to the last minute. While it's fun to be spontaneous and plan some parties and special meals on a moment's notice, leaving too many details to the last minute can lead to frustration.

This book lets you start several months ahead with early preparation of Christmas pudding, fruitcakes and mincemeat. All these improve with aging. Cooking them ahead will help immensely to ease the pressure of those last hectic few days. This chapter also covers the preparation of icing and marzipan decorations, a project too time-consuming to do at the last minute. This job is an ideal one to get out of the way early, and the decorations will keep for several months. Mince pies can also be made ahead and frozen until needed. There are also directions for serving them when they are needed. Other recipes are given for basic pastries that can be prepared and frozen. Don't forget to make cookies ahead, too!

Remember to label foods to be frozen. The label should include the date the food was frozen, recipe name, number of servings and a use-by date. If desired, include the cookbook name and page number or instructions for finishing the dish.

## 12 DAYS OF CHRISTMAS

Traditionally, Christmas is spread over twelve days, beginning on Christmas Eve and ending on January 6th, Twelfth Night. According to tradition, this is the day decorations must be taken down or bad luck will befall the house. In the middle of this period is the New Year, always a good excuse for a party. Whether you have only one or two days off or are lucky enough to have an extended holiday covering the whole period, food is likely to play a large part in your celebrations. Planning your menus day by day can be a tremendous help. Much of the shopping can also be done ahead. The suggestions for menus for the twelve days are designed to cover every situation. They provide ideas for starters, main courses, vegetable accompaniments and desserts for every occasion.

## TURKEY LEFTOVERS

The problem of turkey leftovers is almost proverbial. Many families cringe at the very thought of them. Others, however, see leftovers as the beginning of many new and exciting meals. Here are some recipes to transform your leftovers quickly and easily into delicious meals.

## ALTERNATIVE MENUS & MAIN DISHES

The current economical price of turkey makes it less of a treat because it can be eaten the year around. This and the advent of more adventurous eating habits make turkey no longer the only possible choice for Christmas dinner, as fixed and unchanging as the date itself. Although it will probably remain the favorite for the majority of people, we have included alternatives for those who like to have something different. Among these are types of game, including venison, partridge and duck, all very rich in flavor. Also included is royal beef-rib roast, England's traditional meat for Christmas before America introduced the turkey. As well, we have considered those who have special reasons for not eating turkey. There is a menu that lists the calories, a vegetarian menu, and a menu based on Salmon en Croûte for those who prefer fish.

## CAKES

In spite of having eaten an enormous meal, everyone is always ready for dessert. This may even be the favorite part of the meal. An English tradition is a rich fruitcake, often covered with marzipan and icing. There are directions for several beautiful designs. For those who don't like fruitcake, recipes for richly frosted chocolate and coffee-flavored cakes are included. These are special cakes that can be decorated to create impressive and delicious desserts for entertaining. There is also a wide selection of lighter fruitcakes, such as Dundee Cake and Light Fruitcake. Also included is a Lemon Cake that can be served with or without icing.

## CHRISTMAS ABROAD

Finally, Christmas is celebrated in its own way in many countries all over the world. In addition to having favorites of their own, several other countries share our traditional foods. Many others have foods and customs that are completely different. The final chapter includes some of these foreign favorites for the Christmas holiday. Add them to your repertoire for an exciting change; there are some delicious discoveries to be made. The Greek New Year's cake has a marvelous flavor and texture. The Christmas pudding from New Zealand has to be tried both on its own and in its very special Maori version with ice cream. The Christmas-Tree Cookies will soon disappear from the tree!

Christmas is a time of joy and families, of giving and receiving and of friendliness and fun. Merry Christmas!

Clockwise from top: Glazed Fruitcake, page 66; Brandy Snaps, page 31; Almond Tuiles, page 50; Bûche de Noël, page 76; Spanish Honey Fritters, page 79

## Granny's Christmas Puddings

1-1/3 cups golden raisins
2-2/3 cups dark raisins
1-1/3 cups currants
1/4 cup chopped mixed
　candied peel
1/2 cup chopped red
　candied cherries
2/3 cup chopped
　blanched almonds
1 cup ground almonds
4 cups fresh bread crumbs
2 carrots, grated
1 medium apple, peeled,
　cored, grated
8 oz. suet, shredded

1/2 teaspoon
　pumpkin-pie spice
Pinch of grated nutmeg
1/2 teaspoon ground
　cinnamon
1-1/4 cups sugar
Grated peel and juice of
　1 large lemon
Grated peel and juice of
　1 large orange
2/3 cup dark corn syrup
4 eggs, beaten
1/4 cup brandy
1/2 cup brown ale

*Originally Christmas puddings were made during the last weekend of November to be eaten the following year. Now it is more usual to make the puddings 3 to 6 months in advance.*

1. In a large bowl, stir all ingredients with a wooden spoon until combined.
2. Grease 3 (4-cup) pudding molds or 6 (2-cup) molds. Fill each mold about 3/4 full. Cut pieces of foil large enough to cover puddings; grease foil. Cover puddings with greased foil; tie securely with kitchen string.
3. Place puddings in large kettles; add enough boiling water to come halfway up sides of molds. Steam large puddings 8 hours and small puddings 6 hours over medium-low heat. Add more boiling water as necessary. Remove pudding from pans; cool on wire racks.
4. Remove foil. Remove cooled puddings from molds. Wrap puddings in plastic wrap; then wrap airtight in foil. Store in a cool, dry place 1 to 3 months before serving, or freeze for longer storage.

5. To serve, return puddings to molds. Cover tops with greased foil; tie with kitchen string. Steam as instructed above 3 to 4 hours to heat through. Remove string and foil. Invert on a serving dish; remove molds. Serve with brandy butter or custard sauce. To flame pudding, warm 3 to 4 tablespoons brandy. Pour warmed brandy over pudding; light brandy. Serve while flaming. Makes 3 large puddings or 6 small puddings. Each large pudding makes 8 servings; small puddings make 4 servings.

**To cook puddings in a pressure cooker:**
Prepare and cover as above. Stand puddings on a rack in a pressure cooker; add 5 to 6 cups boiling water. Follow manufacturer's instructions. After pressure is reached; cook large puddings 3 hours and small puddings 2-1/4 hours. Reduce pressure, following instructions; remove pudding. Cool and store as above. To serve, pressure cook a large pudding 1 hour and a small pudding 45 minutes.

## Christmas Puddings

1 cup self-rising flour
3 cups fresh bread crumbs
1 cup currants
1 cup golden raisins
3/4 cup chopped pitted
　dates
1-1/4 cups dark raisins
6 oz. suet, shredded
1/4 cup chopped mixed
　candied peel
1/3 cup chopped
　blanched almonds
1 small apple, peeled,
　cored, grated

Grated peel and juice of
　1 small orange
1/2 teaspoon
　pumpkin-pie spice
1/4 teaspoon grated
　nutmeg
1/2 teaspoon salt
3 eggs
1/4 cup brown ale or
　apple cider
1 cup firmly packed
　dark-brown sugar

1. Grease a 4-cup pudding mold and a 2-cup pudding mold. In a large bowl, stir all ingredients with a wooden spoon until combined. Spoon mixture into greased pudding molds. Cover as directed for Granny's Christmas Puddings.
2. Steam or cook in a pressure cooker as directed for Granny's Christmas Puddings. Cool, wrap and store as directed. To serve, follow directions for Granny's Christmas Puddings. Makes about 12 servings.

*Stages in making Granny's Christmas Pudding*

# Mincemeat Tart

2-1/2 cups Mincemeat
   or Freezer Mincemeat,
   opposite
1/4 cup chopped candied
   cherries
1/4 cup finely chopped
   blanched almonds
2 tablespoons brandy
   or rum

1 (17-1/2-oz) pkg. frozen
   puff pastry (2 sheets),
   thawed
2 tablespoons milk for
   glaze
About 3 tablespoons
   sugar

1. Preheat oven to 425F (220C). In a medium bowl, combine mincemeat, cherries, almonds and brandy or rum; set aside.
2. Unfold 1 pastry sheet on a lightly floured surface. Roll out pastry to an 11" x 9" rectangle. Repeat with second pastry sheet.
3. Place 1 pastry sheet on an ungreased baking sheet. Spread filling over pastry to within 3/4 inch of each edge.
4. Fold second pastry sheet in half lengthwise. Using a floured sharp knife, cut pastry every 1/2 inch, cutting across pastry through fold to within 3/4 inch of unfolded edge. Place over filling with fold at center; unfold pastry.
5. Press pastry edges together to seal. Using blunt edge of a flat-bladed knife and your fingers, flute pastry at 3/4-inch intervals.
6. Brush top with milk; sprinkle lightly with sugar.
7. Bake in preheated oven 25 to 30 minutes or until pastry is golden brown. To serve, cut into slices. Serve hot or cold with ice cream or whipped cream, if desired. Makes 8 to 10 servings.

**To make ahead,** complete through step 7. Cool on baking sheet. Open freeze. Wrap frozen pastry in foil; freeze up to 2 months. **To serve,** place frozen tart on a baking sheet. Heat in preheated 375F (190C) oven about 25 minutes or until warm.

---

### Open Freezing

Open freeze foods, such as tarts or frosted cakes, that are difficult to wrap before freezing. Place unwrapped items on a baking sheet. Freeze until firm. Place frozen items in plastic freezer bags or rigid freezer containers or wrap in foil.

---

# Mincemeat

1 (1-lb.) box currants
   (2 cups)
2 (1-lb.) boxes raisins
   (4 cups), chopped
1 lb. chopped mixed
   candied peel (2 cups)
1 cup finely chopped
   blanched almonds
   (about 4 oz.)
2 lb. apples (about
   6 medium), peeled,
   cored, coarsely grated
2 (1-lb.) boxes
   dark-brown sugar

1 lb. ground beef, cooked
8 oz. suet, shredded
1 teaspoon grated
   nutmeg
1 teaspoon ground
   cinnamon
1 teaspoon pumpkin-pie
   spice
Grated peel of 2 lemons
Juice of 1 lemon
2 to 4 tablespoons brandy

1. In a large bowl, combine currants, raisins, candied peel and almonds. Stir in apples, brown sugar, beef, suet, spices, lemon peel and lemon juice until combined.
2. Cover bowl with plastic wrap; refrigerate overnight.
3. Pour mixture into a large kettle. Bring to a boil over medium heat; boil 10 minutes, stirring occasionally. Remove from heat; stir in brandy. Pack hot mincemeat into hot 1-pint or 1-quart canning jars. Seal with canning lids, following manufacturer's directions. Process in a pressure cooker according to manufacturer's directions. Makes about 6 quarts.

# Freezer Mincemeat

2 lb. apples (about
   6 medium), peeled,
   cored, finely chopped
1-1/2 cups currants
1-1/2 cups golden raisins
1-1/2 cups dark raisins,
   chopped
1 cup chopped mixed
   candied peel
3/4 cup chopped
   blanched almonds

1 (1-lb.) box dark-brown
   sugar
4 oz. suet, shredded
1 teaspoon grated
   nutmeg
1 teaspoon ground
   cinnamon
Grated peel of 1 orange
Grated peel and juice of
   1 lemon
2 cups apple juice

1. In a large kettle, combine all ingredients. Cook over low heat, stirring until sugar is dissolved. Simmer 1 hour, stirring frequently. Cool slightly; refrigerate until chilled. Or, pour into a large bowl; place bowl in a sink of iced water. Stir occasionally to cool quickly.
2. Spoon cooled mixture into plastic containers or small plastic freezer bags in 1 cup amounts. Freeze up to 3 months. Thaw overnight in refrigerator before using. Makes about 10 cups.

# Mince Tarts

| | |
|---|---|
| 3 recipes Shortcrust Pastry, page 16 | 2 tablespoons milk |
| 3 cups Mincemeat or Freezer Mincemeat, opposite | About 3 tablespoons sugar |

**1.** Preheat oven to 400F (205C). Prepare pastry as directed on page 16. Divide pastry in half. On a lightly floured surface, roll out 1/2 of pastry to 1/4 inch thick. With a fluted 3-inch round cutter, cut out 12 circles. Roll out remaining dough; cut out 12 (2-1/2-inch) circles.

**2.** Use large circles to line 2-1/2-inch tart pans. Fill each with 1/4 cup mincemeat. Dampen pastry edges; top each tart with a small circle. Press edges to seal.

**3.** Brush tops of tarts with milk; sprinkle lightly with sugar. Make a small hole in top of each tart to allow steam to escape.

**4.** Bake in preheated oven about 20 minutes or until golden brown. Cool in pans on wire racks 10 minutes. Carefully remove from pans; cool completely on wire racks. Makes 12 tarts.

**To make ahead,** complete through step 4. Place cooled tarts on a baking sheet; open freeze. Pack in plastic freezer bags or plastic freezer containers. Freeze up to 2 months.
**To serve,** place frozen tarts on a baking sheet. Bake in preheated 375F (190C) oven about 25 minutes or until hot.

Mincemeat Tart

# Christmas Cake

1 cup butter or
   margarine, room
   temperature
2 cups firmly packed
   dark-brown sugar
4 eggs
2 tablespoons molasses
1 tablespoon lemon juice
   or orange juice
1-1/2 cups all-purpose
   flour, sifted
1 teaspoon pumpkin-pie
   spice
1/2 teaspoon ground
   cinnamon
1/4 teaspoon ground
   mace or nutmeg
1 cup dark raisins
1 cup golden raisins
2 cups currants
1/2 cup chopped mixed
   candied fruit
1/2 cup chopped
   blanched almonds
1/2 cup red candied
   cherries, quartered
Grated peel of 1 lemon
Grated peel of 1 small
   orange
3 to 4 tablespoons brandy

**1.** Preheat oven to 300F (150C). Grease a deep 8-inch-round cake pan or springform pan. Line side and bottom of pan with waxed paper; grease paper.
**2.** In a large bowl, beat butter or margarine and brown sugar until light and fluffy. Beat in eggs, 1 at a time, beating well after each addition. Stir in molasses and juice.
**3.** Sift flour and spices over egg mixture; fold in with a large heavy spoon.
**4.** In a large bowl, combine raisins, currants, candied fruit, almonds, cherries, lemon peel and orange peel. Stir into batter until distributed. Spoon into prepared pan; smooth top.
**5.** Bake in preheated oven 2-1/2 to 3 hours or until a skewer inserted into center comes out clean.
**6.** Cool completely in pan. Remove cake from pan. Remove paper. Spoon brandy over cake; let soak in. Wrap cake in waxed paper. Wrap in foil. Store in a cool, dry place 1 to 3 months before serving, or freeze for longer storage. Makes 10 to 12 servings.

# Christmas Cake with Dates

3/4 cup butter or
   margarine, room
   temperature
1 cup firmly packed
   dark-brown sugar
3 eggs
3 tablespoons molasses
2 teaspoons grated lemon
   peel
1 cup currants
1 cup dark raisins
3/4 cup golden raisins
1/2 cup chopped pitted
   dates
1/3 cup red candied
   cherries, quartered
1/4 cup chopped mixed
   candied fruit
1-3/4 cups sifted
   all-purpose flour
1/2 teaspoon ground
   cinnamon
1/4 teaspoon freshly
   grated nutmeg
1/4 teaspoon ground
   cloves
2 tablespoons lemon juice
2 tablespoons brandy

**1.** Preheat oven to 300F (150C). Grease a deep 8-inch-round cake pan or springform pan. Line bottom and side of pan with parchment paper, extending paper 1 inch above rim of pan.
**2.** In a large bowl, beat butter or margarine and brown sugar until light and fluffy. Beat in eggs, 1 at a time, beating well after each addition. Beat in molasses and lemon peel until blended.
**3.** In a large bowl, combine currants, raisins, dates, cherries and candied fruit. Stir into egg mixture until distributed.
**4.** Sift flour, cinnamon, nutmeg and cloves over fruit mixture; fold in. Add lemon juice and brandy; stir until blended. Spoon mixture into prepared pan; smooth top.
**5.** Bake in preheated oven 2-1/2 hours or until skewer inserted in center comes out clean. Cool completely in pan on a wire rack. Remove from pan; peel off paper. Wrap cake in waxed paper. Wrap with foil. Store in a cool, dry place 1 to 3 months before serving, or freeze for longer storage. Makes 12 to 16 servings.

Left to right: Christmas Cake, Christmas Cake with Dates

## Christmas-Cake Decorations

These decorations can be made 3 to 8 weeks ahead. If made from a dark-colored marzipan, they must be made at least a week in advance. This is to allow for drying time; otherwise the color will spoil white icing. Either make your own marzipan, page 70, or if time is short, buy prepared marzipan or almond paste.

Use a good-quality food coloring for coloring marzipan or icing. Special pastes and powders are available for really deep colors. Experiment with mixing colors, too. Knead coloring into marzipan or fondant icing until color is even and no streaks remain. Add color to Royal Icing by dipping a skewer into coloring; just touch to icing to avoid over-coloring. White icings are easiest to color. A commercial almost-white marzipan is available which is also ideal for coloring. Paint extra color on marzipan and icing flowers and leaves with liquid food colorings and a very fine paint brush.

### Rolled Marzipan

Roll out marzipan between two sheets of plastic wrap or waxed paper. This is an easy method that gives an even result. When completely dry, store marzipan decorations in airtight containers with waxed paper or plastic wrap between each layer. Stored in this way, marzipan decorations will keep up to two months.

**Holly Leaves & Berries**—Make a dark-green marzipan by kneading green, blue and a touch of brown food coloring into marzipan. Roll out thinly; cut into rectangles 1 to 1-1/2 inches long and 3/4 inch wide. Using a tiny round aspic cutter, petit-fours cutter or base of a piping tip, make leaves by taking cuts out of edges of marzipan rectangles. With a sharp knife, make a vein down center of each one. Let dry on parchment paper. Or, lay over a lightly greased wooden-spoon handle for curved leaves. For berries, tint a small piece of marzipan deep red. Shape into tiny balls, rolling them between palms of your hands. Let stand at room temperature 24 hours or until completely dry. Store up to 2 months.

**Christmas Trees**—On a piece of waxed paper, draw a pattern of a simple Christmas tree in size desired. Using pattern as a guide, cut out Christmas trees from thinly rolled green marzipan; let stand until completely dry. A base may be made from red marzipan. For decorations, apply tiny silver dragrees to tips of branches with a dab of icing. Store up to 2 months.

**Ivy Leaves & Mistletoe**—On a piece of waxed paper, draw several sizes of patterns for ivy leaves and mistletoe leaves. Cut mistletoe leaves from thinly rolled pale-green marzipan. Cut ivy leaves from thinly rolled medium-green marzipan. With a sharp knife, mark veins; let stand until completely dry. Make mistletoe berries, which are larger than holly berries, from white marzipan. Store up to 2 months.

### Molded Marzipan or Fondant-Icing Flowers

**Roses**—Roll out marzipan or fondant icing very thinly. For each flower cut 2 (1/2-inch) circles. Hold a circle between thumb and finger. With fingers of other hand, carefully press out rest of circle until very thin and almost transparent. Using thick part as base of rose, roll for center of rose. Wrap another circle around the first. Wrap tightly at base, but leave edge loose at top to show center. If using fondant icing, use a little water to make petals stick firmly. Continue with three or four more circles to make petals. Make each a little looser than previous one; attach to base in same way. For a small rose, four petals are enough. A larger rose may need seven or eight petals. Let dry on parchment paper on a wire rack up to a week before storing carefully between layers of plastic wrap or waxed paper in an airtight container. Store up to 2 months.

**Christmas Roses**—Make these by molding small pieces of marzipan or fondant icing into petals with rounded tips

Piped, rolled and molded decorations

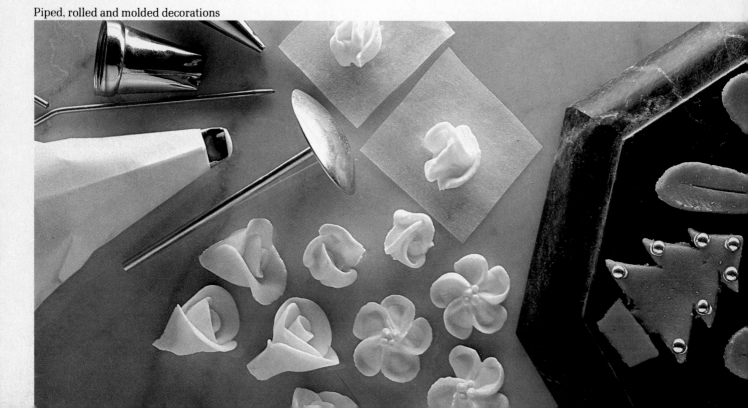

and slightly upturned edges. Place petals, slightly overlapping, in groups of five for each rose. Press non-rounded edges together to form center; see photo opposite. Fill center with tiny yellow marzipan balls or fondant icing. Or pipe dots of yellow royal icing for stamens. Let dry completely in a cool place before storing in layers in an airtight container. Store up to 2 months.

### Piped Royal-Icing Flowers

To make icing flowers, you will need an icing nail or a cork impaled on a small skewer, a quantity of waxed paper cut into 1-1/2-inch squares and a paper or plastic pastry bag fitted with a medium petal tip. Half-fill pastry bag with *Royal Icing*, page 70. Color icing to desired color. Store up to 2 months.

**Roses**—Attach a paper square to icing nail with a dab of icing. Hold pastry bag so the thin edge of petal tip faces up. Squeezing pastry bag gently and evenly and twisting nail at same time, pipe a tight coil for center of rose. Continue to add 5 or 6 petals, one at a time, piping icing and twisting nail at same time. Pipe each petal only about three-fourths of the way around flower. Begin in a different part of flower each time to keep shape even. Hold tip in towards center of flower to prevent rose expanding at base and top and losing its shape. The petals can be kept tight to form a rosebud or more open for full-blown flowers. Let dry completely on parchment paper; when dry, store in an airtight container. If icing roses are damp when stored, they will mold. Store up to 2 months.

**Christmas Roses**—This is a flat flower that should be made with white icing. Begin with the thick edge of the petal tip in the center of the icing nail. Keep the tip horizontal and form each petal separately. Gently squeeze out the icing. Move tip out, making a rounded point, keeping petals slightly tilted up at the edges. Then bring it back toward the center, twisting it slightly and gradually releasing the pressure. This give a single petal. Make four more petals in the same way to give an even flower, making each one slightly overlap its neighbor by placing the tip just under the previous petal as you begin to pipe. Let dry completely on parchment paper. Pipe pale yellow icing dots in the center for stamens. Let dry completely before storing. Store up to 2 months.

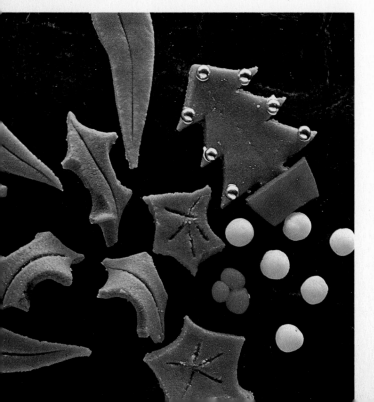

# Shortcrust Pastry

| | |
|---|---|
| 1-1/2 cups all-purpose flour | 1/4 cup vegetable shortening |
| 1/2 teaspoon salt | 3 or 4 tablespoons iced water |
| 1/4 cup butter or margarine | |

**1.** In a medium bowl, combine flour and salt. With a pastry blender or 2 knives, cut in butter or margarine and shortening until mixture resembles coarse crumbs.
**2.** Sprinkle with iced water, 1 tablespoon at a time; toss with a fork until mixture binds together. Knead in bowl 8 to 10 strokes or until smooth.
**3.** Shape pastry into a flattened ball. Roll, fill and bake as directed in recipe. Makes enough pastry for a 9- or 10-inch single crust pie.

**To make ahead,** complete through step 3. Wrap in plastic wrap; wrap in foil or place in a plastic freezer bag. Freeze up to 2 months. **To use,** thaw at room temperature 2 hours or in refrigerator overnight.

# Puff Pastry

| | |
|---|---|
| 4 cups sifted all-purpose flour | 1 tablespoon lemon juice |
| 1 teaspoon salt | 1-1/4 cups iced water |
| 2 cups butter or margarine, chilled | |

**1.** Sift flour and salt into a medium bowl. With a pastry blender or 2 knives, cut in 6 tablespoons butter or margarine. Stir in lemon juice and water to make a soft dough. Knead dough in bowl several strokes or until smooth.
**2.** On a lightly floured surface, roll out dough to a 12-inch square. Shape remaining butter or margarine into a 10" x 5" rectangle. Place butter or margarine rectangle on 1 side of pastry square, leaving a 1-inch border. Fold remaining pastry over butter or margarine, enclosing completely. Press edges to seal.
**3.** Roll pastry with a rolling pin several times, rolling out pastry to a 24" x 8" rectangle. Fold into thirds. Wrap in waxed paper or plastic wrap; refrigerate 30 minutes.
**4.** Repeat rolling, folding and chilling 5 times.
**5.** Wrap and refrigerate pastry at least 1 hour before using. Roll, fill and bake as directed in recipe. Makes about 2 pounds of pastry.

**To make ahead,** complete through step 4. Cut pastry in half. Wrap each piece in foil; place in a plastic freezer bag. Freeze up to 2 months. **To use,** thaw at room temperature 2 to 3 hours or overnight in refrigerator.

# Choux Paste

| | |
|---|---|
| 1/2 cup butter or margarine | 1/4 teaspoon salt |
| 1 cup water | 1 cup sifted all-purpose flour |
| 1 tablespoon sugar | 4 eggs |

**1.** Preheat oven to 400F (205C). Grease 2 baking sheets.
**2.** In a medium saucepan over medium heat, combine butter or margarine, water, sugar and salt; bring to a boil. Add flour all at once. Stir with a wooden spoon until dough forms a ball and comes away from side of pan. Cool slightly.
**3.** Beat in eggs, 1 at a time, beating well after each addition.
**4. To make Cream Puffs,** spoon dough into a pastry bag fitted with a large plain tip. Pipe 24 small balls about 2 inches apart on greased baking sheets.

Stuffing ingredients

**5.** Bake in preheated oven 25 to 30 minutes or until puffed and golden brown. Remove from baking sheets; cut a small slit in side of each cream puff to let steam escape. Cool completely on wire racks.

**6.** Cut tops off cream puffs. Remove and discard soft interior. Fill with favorite filling. Replace tops. Makes 24 cream puffs.

**To make ahead,** complete through step 5. Place cooled cream puffs in a plastic freezer container. Freeze up to 2 months. **To serve,** thaw at room temperature. Heat in a preheated 375F (190C) oven about 5 minutes to crisp; cool before filling.

## Apricot & Apple Stuffing

| | |
|---|---|
| 1/4 cup finely chopped dried apricots | 1-1/2 cups fresh bread crumbs |
| 1 tablespoon vegetable oil | Salt |
| 1 small onion, finely chopped | Freshly ground pepper |
| 2 celery stalks, finely chopped | 3 bacon slices, crisp-cooked, crumbled |
| 1 apple, peeled, cored, finely chopped | 2 tablespoons lemon juice |
| | 1 egg yolk |

**1.** Place apricots in a small bowl; cover with boiling water. Let stand 2 to 3 hours. Drain well.
**2.** Heat oil in a medium skillet over medium heat. Add onion and celery; sauté 2 to 3 minutes or until softened. Stir in apple; cook 2 to 3 minutes or until apple is softened.
**3.** In a medium bowl, combine drained apricots, onion mixture and bread crumbs. Season with salt and pepper.
**4.** Stir in bacon, lemon juice and egg yolk until combined. Makes enough stuffing for a 10- to 12-pound turkey.

**To make ahead,** complete through step 3. Cover and refrigerate overnight. Or, package and freeze up to 1 month. **To use,** thaw in refrigerator overnight, if frozen. Complete step 4.

## Walnut, Orange & Coriander Stuffing

| | |
|---|---|
| 2 tablespoons butter or margarine | 2-1/2 cups fresh bread crumbs |
| 1 onion, chopped | Salt |
| 2 teaspoons ground coriander | Freshly ground pepper |
| Grated peel of 1 orange | 1 egg, beaten |
| 1/4 cup finely chopped walnuts | 2 tablespoons orange juice |
| 1/2 cup coarsely chopped raisins | 2 tablespoons chopped fresh parsley |

**1.** Melt butter or margarine in a medium skillet over low heat. Add onion; sauté about 10 minutes or until soft and golden brown. Spoon cooked onions into a medium bowl. Stir in coriander, orange peel, walnuts, raisins and bread crumbs until combined. Season with salt and pepper.
**2.** Stir in egg and orange juice until combined. Stir in parsley. Makes enough stuffing for a 10- to 12-pound turkey.

**To make ahead,** complete through step 1. Cover and refrigerate overnight. Or, package and freeze up to 1 month. **To use,** thaw overnight in refrigerator overnight, if frozen; complete step 2.

# Smoked-Salmon & Asparagus Quiche

| | |
|---|---|
| 1 recipe Shortcrust Pastry, page 16 | 3 eggs |
| 6 oz. smoked-salmon trimmings, coarsely chopped | 1-1/4 cups half and half |
| | Freshly ground pepper |
| 1 (15-oz.) can asparagus spears, drained | 1/2 cup shredded Cheddar cheese (2 oz.) |
| | 1/2 cup fresh bread crumbs |

1. Preheat oven to 375 (190C). Prepare pastry as directed on page 16. On a lightly floured surface, roll out pastry to an 11-inch circle. Use pastry to line a 9- or 10-inch flan pan or pie pan. Crimp or flute pastry edge; prick bottom with a fork. Line pastry with foil; fill with pie weights or dried beans.

2. Bake in preheated oven 15 minutes. Remove foil and pie weights or beans; bake 5 to 8 minutes or until golden.

3. Arrange smoked salmon in pastry. Reserve tips of 6 asparagus spears for garnish. Chop remaining asparagus; arrange over salmon.

4. In a medium bowl, beat eggs and half and half. Season with pepper. Pour mixture over asparagus and salmon. In a small bowl, combine cheese and crumbs; sprinkle evenly over surface.

5. Bake in preheated oven 35 to 40 minutes or until puffed and top is golden brown. Garnish with reserved asparagus. Makes 6 servings.

**Variation**
Garnish with tiny rolls of smoked salmon.

**To make ahead,** complete through step 5. Refrigerate until cool. Place on a baking sheet; open freeze. Wrap in foil; freeze up to 1 month. **To serve,** thaw overnight in refrigerator. Serve cold or heat in preheated 375F (190C) oven about 20 minutes or until heated through.

# Pissaladière

| | |
|---|---|
| 1 recipe Shortcrust Pastry, page 16 | 2 (15-oz.) cans tomatoes, drained |
| 3 tablespoons vegetable oil | 1/2 cup shredded Cheddar cheese (2 oz.) |
| 2 large onions, thinly sliced | 1 (2-oz.) can anchovy fillets, drained, halved lengthwise |
| 2 or 3 garlic cloves, crushed | |
| Salt | *To garnish:* |
| Freshly ground pepper | Black olives |

1. Preheat oven to 400F (205C). Prepare pastry as directed on page 16. On a lightly floured surface, roll out pastry to an 11-inch circle. Use pastry to line a 9- or 10-inch flan pan or pie pan. Crimp or flute pastry edge; prick bottom with a fork. Line pastry with foil; fill with pie weights or dried beans.

2. Bake in preheated oven 15 minutes. Remove foil and pie weights or beans; bake 5 to 8 minutes or until golden. Set aside. Reduce oven temperature to 375F (190C).

3. Heat oil in a medium skillet. Add onions and garlic; sauté over low heat about 5 minutes or until soft and lightly browned. Cool slightly.

4. Spoon onion mixture into pastry shell; season with salt and pepper.

5. Coarsely chop tomatoes. Spoon chopped tomatoes over onions; sprinkle with cheese. Arrange anchovy fillets in a lattice pattern over cheese. Place an olive in each lattice square.

6. Bake in preheated oven about 20 minutes or until filling is hot. Serve warm. Makes 6 servings.

**To make ahead,** complete through step 6. Refrigerate baked tart until cool. Place on a baking sheet; open freeze. Wrap in foil; freeze up to 1 month. **To serve,** thaw overnight in refrigerator. Serve cold or heat in a preheated 400F (205C) oven 15 minutes or until hot.

# Buttercream Frosting

| | |
|---|---|
| 1/4 cup butter or margarine, room temperature | 1 teaspoon vanilla extract |
| | 1 to 2 tablespoons milk |
| 1 cup powdered sugar, sifted | |

1. In a small bowl, beat butter or margarine until creamy. Beat in powdered sugar until fluffy.

2. Beat in vanilla and 1 tablespoon milk until frosting is a good consistency for spreading, beating in more milk if necessary. Makes about 1 cup.

# Easy Butter Cookies

**Cookies:**

| | |
|---|---|
| 1 cup butter, room temperature | 3/4 finely chopped pecans |
| 2/3 cup sugar | *To decorate:* |
| 1 egg yolk | **Buttercream Frosting, opposite** |
| 2 teaspoons vanilla extract | **Green and red candied cherries** |
| 1-3/4 cups all-purpose flour | |

**1.** Preheat oven to 350F (175C). To make cookies, in a medium bowl, beat butter, sugar, egg yolk and vanilla until light and fluffy. Gradually beat in flour and pecans until blended.

**2.** Drop dough by teaspoons 2 inches apart on ungreased baking sheets.

**3.** Bake in preheated oven 12 to 15 minutes or until lightly browned. Cool on baking sheets on wire racks 5 minutes. Remove from baking sheets; cool completely on wire racks.

**4.** To decorate, spoon Buttercream Frosting into a pastry bag fitted with a star or rosette tip. Pipe a rosette in center of each cookie. Decorate with cherries. Let stand until frosting is set. Makes about 40 cookies.

**To make ahead,** complete through step 3. Place cooled, undecorated cookies in plastic freezer containers. Freeze up to 1 month. **To serve,** thaw at room temperature. Decorate before serving.

Left to right: Smoked-Salmon & Asparagus Quiche, Pissaladière

# Dundee Cake

| | |
|---|---|
| 1/2 cup chopped blanched almonds | 1 cup butter or margarine |
| 1-1/4 cup currants | 1-1/3 cups firmly packed dark-brown sugar |
| 1-1/2 cup golden raisins | 5 eggs |
| 1-1/2 cups dark raisins | 2 cups all-purpose flour |
| 1/2 cup chopped mixed candied fruit | 1 teaspoon pumpkin-pie spice |
| Grated peel of 1 orange | 1/2 cup whole blanched almonds |
| Grated peel of 1 lemon | |

*This is lighter than a traditional Christmas cake. It is always topped with whole blanched almonds before baking. If desired, pierce with a skewer; sprinkle with 3 to 4 tablespoons brandy before wrapping in plastic wrap and foil. Dundee cake can be made 2 to 3 weeks before serving or up to 4 months ahead, if frozen.*

**1.** Preheat oven to 300F (150C). Grease a deep 8-inch-round cake pan or springform pan. Line side and bottom with a double thickness of waxed paper; grease paper.
**2.** In a medium bowl, combine chopped almonds, currants, raisins, candied fruit, orange peel and lemon peel.
**3.** In a large bowl, beat butter or margarine and sugar until light and fluffy. Beat in eggs, 1 at a time, beating well after each addition.
**4.** Sift flour and spice over egg mixture; fold in. Stir in fruit mixture until distributed. Spoon mixture into prepared pan; smooth top. Arrange whole blanched almonds in circles over top of cake.
**5.** Bake in preheated oven 2 to 2-1/2 hours or until a skewer inserted into center comes out clean. Cover cake with foil if almonds brown too quickly.
**6.** Cool in pan on a wire rack about 15 minutes. Remove from pan; remove paper. Cool completely on wire rack. Wrap cooled cake in plastic wrap; wrap in foil. Store in a cool, dry place up to 2 weeks, or freeze up to 4 months. Makes 10 to 12 servings.

---

### Marzipan-Filled Fruit

Fill pitted dates, candied cherries or prunes with small pieces of marzipan. Crisscross top of marzipan with a small sharp knife; see photo opposite. Roll filled fruit in sugar, if desired.

---

# Almond Macaroons

| | |
|---|---|
| 2 egg whites | 1-1/3 cups finely ground blanched almonds |
| 1/3 cup sugar | Red and green candied cherries, chopped |
| 1/2 teaspoon almond extract | |

**1.** Preheat oven to 300F (150C). Line 2 baking sheets with parchment paper.
**2.** Beat egg whites in a medium bowl until stiff but not dry. Beat in sugar, 1 tablespoon at a time; beat until meringue is stiff and glossy.
**3.** Fold in almond extract and ground almonds. Spoon mixture into a pastry bag fitted with a 1/2-inch open star tip. Pipe mixture in small stars about 1 inch apart on lined baking sheets. Decorate with chopped candied cherries.
**4.** Bake in preheated oven 15 to 17 minutes or until lightly browned. Carefully remove from paper; cool completely on wire racks. Store in an airtight container until served. Makes 18 cookies.

**To make ahead,** complete through step 4. Place cooled cookies in plastic freezer containers. Freeze up to 2 weeks. **To serve,** thaw at room temperature.

# Rum Truffles

| | |
|---|---|
| 4 oz. semisweet chocolate, chopped | 2 teaspoons rum |
| 2-1/3 cups powdered sugar, sifted | Chocolate sprinkles |
| 1/2 cup butter or margarine, room temperature | |

**1.** Melt chocolate in a small heavy saucepan over very low heat; stir until smooth. Remove from heat. Gradually stir in powdered sugar and butter or margarine until smooth. Stir in rum.
**2.** Shape mixture into walnut-sized balls; roll 1/2 of balls in chocolate sprinkles. Place on waxed paper; let stand 4 to 5 hours to set.
**3.** Serve in paper cases. Makes 1 pound.

**To make ahead,** complete through step 2. Store in an airtight container up to 2 weeks. **To serve,** arrange in paper cases.

# Orange-Cranberry Relish

**1 lb. fresh cranberries**
   **(about 4 cups)**
**1-1/2 cups sugar**
**1 cup water**
**Grated peel of 1 orange**
**2 tablespoons**
   **orange-flavored liqueur**

**1/2 cup finely chopped**
   **almonds, walnuts or**
   **pecans**
**1/2 cup raisins, if desired**
**1/4 cup finely chopped**
   **celery**

**1.** Rinse cranberries under cold running water; discard stems and any shriveled cranberries.

**2.** Place cranberries, sugar and water in a medium saucepan. Cook over medium heat, stirring occasionally, until mixture comes to a boil. Reduce heat; simmer 5 minutes or until skins begin to pop, skimming surface as necessary. Remove from heat; cool completely.

**3.** Pour cranberries into a serving bowl. Stir in orange peel, liqueur, nuts, raisins and celery. Cover and refrigerate until served. Makes about 4 cups.

**To make ahead,** complete through step 2. Cover and refrigerate up to 1 week. **To serve,** complete step 3.

Clockwise from bottom: Almond Macaroons, Marzipan-Filled Fruit, Rum Truffles, Dundee Cake

*Christmas Eve*

Beef & Chicken Casserole*
Steamed Rice
Creamy Coleslaw
Relish Tray
Mincemeat & Apple Pie*

*Recipe included in book

## Mincemeat & Apple Pie

2 recipes Shortcrust
  Pastry, page 16
1 lb. apples (3 medium),
  peeled, cored, sliced
1 cup mincemeat
2 tablespoons brandy,
  if desired

2 tablespoons apricot jam
2 teaspoons water
About 2 tablespoons milk
Whipped cream,
  if desired

**1.** Preheat oven to 400F (205C). Prepare pastry as directed on page 16. Divide in half. On a lightly floured surface, roll out 1 piece of dough to a 10-inch circle. Use pastry to line a 9-inch pie pan. Reserve remaining pastry.
**2.** Arrange 1/2 of apple slices in pastry shell. Cover evenly with mincemeat; sprinkle with brandy, if desired. Arrange remaining apple slices over mincemeat.
**3.** In a small saucepan over low heat, heat apricot jam and water. Stir until jam melts. Brush mixture over apples.
**4.** Roll out reserved pastry; cut into narrow strips. Twist strips; arrange over apples. Moisten ends of strips; press to pastry rim to seal. Flute edges. Brush pastry strips and rim with milk.
**5.** Bake in preheated oven about 35 minutes or until pastry is golden brown. Serve hot or cold with whipped cream. Makes 6 servings.

## Beef & Chicken Casserole

2 tablespoons vegetable
  oil
1 (2-1/2-lb.) chicken, cut
  into serving pieces
1 lb. beef for stew, cut
  into 1-inch cubes
2 large onions, peeled,
  cut into eighths
2 tablespoons all-purpose
  flour

1/2 cup dry white wine
1-1/2 cups beef stock
1 tablespoon red-wine
  vinegar
Salt
Freshly ground pepper
1/2 teaspoon dried leaf
  thyme
1/4 cup cranberry sauce
4 oz. mushrooms, sliced

**1.** Heat oil in a medium skillet over medium heat. Add chicken; sauté until browned on all sides. Use tongs to transfer chicken to a casserole.
**2.** Add beef to oil remaining in skillet; sauté until browned on all sides. Add to casserole.
**3.** Add onions to skillet; sauté until lightly browned. Stir in flour; cook 1 minute, stirring. Gradually stir in wine, stock and vinegar; bring to a boil. Season with salt and pepper. Stir in thyme and cranberry sauce; stir until sauce melts. Spoon mixture into casserole. Cover with a lid or foil.
**4.** Bake in 325F (165C) oven 1-1/2 hours. Stir in mushrooms; cook 30 minutes more or until chicken and beef are tender. Serve with steamed rice. Makes 6 servings.

Left to right: Mincemeat & Apple Pie, Beef & Chicken Casserole

## Christmas Day

Roast Turkey & Stuffing*
Gravy
Steamed Brussels Sprouts
Orange-Cranberry Relish*
Brown-Sugar Meringues*
Christmas Pudding*

*Recipe included in book

## Roast Turkey & Stuffing

1 (10- to 12-lb.)
   oven-ready turkey,
   with giblets
1 small onion, peeled,
   quartered
Apple & Apricot Stuffing,
   page 17
3 tablespoons butter or
   margarine, softened
2 tablespoons vegetable
   oil
Salt
Freshly ground black
   pepper

*To serve:*
Gravy, if desired
Oven-roasted potatoes
1 lb. small sausages,
   broiled
8 to 16 rolled bacon
   slices, broiled

*To garnish:*
Watercress or parsley
   sprigs

**1.** In a medium saucepan, combine giblets and onion; cover with cold water. Bring to a boil; reduce heat. Cover and simmer 1 hour. Strain stock; cool slightly. Refrigerate until needed for gravy.
**2.** Preheat oven to 350F (175C). Stuff turkey with stuffing. Secure neck skin with a skewer; lightly truss stuffed turkey.
**3.** Place turkey on a rack in a roasting pan; rub all over with butter or margarine. Season turkey with salt and pepper.
**4.** Roast in preheated oven about 3-1/2 hours or until a thermometer inserted in inner thigh area, without touching bone, reads 180F (85C). Juices will be clear when pierced with a skewer in inner thigh area. Baste occasionally with pan drippings while roasting.
**5.** Transfer turkey to a large platter. Remove fat from pan drippings. Remove fat from reserved stock. Thicken drippings and stock with cornstarch to make gravy, if desired.
**6.** Arrange oven-roasted potatoes, sausages and bacon rolls around turkey. Garnish with watercress or parsley. Makes 8 servings.

## Brown-Sugar Meringues

4 egg whites
1/2 cup granulated sugar
1/2 cup firmly packed
   light-brown sugar

1/2 pint whipping cream
   (1 cup), if desired,
   whipped

**1.** Preheat oven to 250F (120C). Line 2 baking sheets with parchment paper. In a medium bowl, beat egg whites until soft peaks form. Gradually beat in sugars until stiff and glossy.

Left to right: Christmas Pudding, page 8; Brown-Sugar Meringues; Steamed Brussels sprouts; Roast Turkey & Stuffing

**2.** Spoon meringue mixture into a pastry bag fitted with a star tip. Pipe into twists or whirls on lined baking sheets.

**3.** Bake in preheated oven about 2 hours or until meringues are firm and dry. Remove from oven; cool completely on baking sheet on wire racks. Carefully peel off paper; store at room temperature in an airtight container up to 2 weeks.

**4.** Immediately before serving, sandwich meringues together with whipped cream, if desired. Makes 20 meringues.

*Boxing Day*
Old-Fashioned Meat Pie*
Potatoes in Cream Sauce*
Winter Salad*
Mince Tarts, page 11
Caramelized Oranges*

*Recipe included in book

## Old-Fashioned Meat Pie

1 recipe Puff Pastry,
   page 16
3 bacon slices, diced
2 lb. beef for stew, cut
   into 1-inch cubes
2 large onions, sliced
3 large carrots, sliced
4 celery stalks, sliced
1 bay leaf
2 cups beef stock
1 cup red wine
Salt
Freshly ground pepper
1 tablespoon cornstarch
2 tablespoons port or
   sherry
3 tablespoons
   red-currant jelly
1 egg, beaten

1. Prepare and chill pastry as directed on page 16.
2. In a large saucepan, sauté bacon until crisp. Remove with a slotted spoon; drain on paper towels. Crumble bacon. Add beef to pan drippings in batches; sauté until browned, stirring occasionally.
3. Return crumbled bacon and sautéed beef to saucepan. Add onions, carrots, celery, bay leaf, stock and wine. Bring to a boil; season with salt and pepper. Cover and simmer 1 to 1-1/2 hours or until beef is tender, stirring occasionally.
4. Preheat oven to 425F (220C). With a slotted spoon, place meat and vegetables in a large casserole, reserving cooking liquid.
5. In a small bowl, combine cornstarch and port or sherry. Stir cornstarch mixture and jelly into cooking liquid. Boil until slightly reduced, stirring constantly. Pour into casserole.
6. On a lightly floured surface, roll out pastry slightly larger than top of casserole. Place pastry over casserole. Trim pastry even with edge of casserole, reserving trimmings; flute pastry.
7. Roll out pastry trimmings; cut into leaves. Brush pastry top with egg; make a hole in center. Arrange pastry leaves around hole. Brush leaves with egg.
8. Bake in preheated oven about 20 minutes. Reduce temperature to 375F (190C); bake 20 to 30 minutes more or until golden brown. Makes 8 servings.

## Winter Salad

2 green-skinned apples
2 red-skinned apples
2 pears
2 tablespoons lemon juice
4 celery stalks, sliced
1/2 cup walnut halves
4 green onions, finely
   sliced
1/4 cup French dressing
2 tablespoons half and
   half

1. Core and slice apples; place in a large bowl. Peel, core and slice pears; add to bowl. Sprinkle with lemon juice. Toss lightly to coat.
2. Add celery, walnuts and onions. In a small bowl, combine French dressing and half and half; pour over salad. Toss lightly to coat with dressing. Cover and refrigerate up to 4 hours. Makes 8 servings.

## Potatoes in Cream Sauce

2-1/2 lb. potatoes (7 or 8
   medium), peeled
Salt
3 tablespoons butter or
   margarine
1/4 cup all-purpose flour
1 cup milk
1/2 cup half and half
Freshly ground white
   pepper
Freshly ground nutmeg
2 tablespoons chopped
   fresh parsley

1. Cut potatoes into 2-inch chunks. In a large saucepan, cook potatoes in salted water until tender. Drain; keep warm.
2. Melt butter or margarine in a medium saucepan over medium heat. Stir in flour; cook 1 minute, stirring. Gradually stir in milk and half and half. Bring to a boil; reduce heat. Simmer 2 minutes. Season with salt, white pepper and nutmeg.
3. Gently stir in potatoes. Spoon into a serving dish; sprinkle with parsley. Makes 8 servings.

# Caramelized Oranges

| 16 medium oranges | 1 cup water |
| 2-1/4 cups sugar | 8 whole cloves |

**1.** Thinly cut peel from 5 oranges; remove bitter white pith. Cut peel into narrow strips; place in a small saucepan. Cover with cold water. Bring to boil; reduce heat. Simmer 10 minutes or until tender. Drain peel, reserving 1/4 cup cooking liquid. Cover and refrigerate peel.

**2.** Cut peel and pith from remaining oranges, reserving any juice. Stand all oranges in a single layer in a bowl.

**3.** In a large heavy saucepan over medium heat, combine sugar, water and cloves. Stir until sugar dissolves. Boil, without stirring, until syrup turns a caramel color. Remove from heat immediately; stir in reser... liquid and any reserved orange juice.

**4.** Return to heat; stir until smooth. Pour hot s... oranges. Cover and refrigerate at least 12 hours a... preferably 1 to 2 days, turning fruit in syrup occasionally.

**5.** To serve, cut each orange crosswise into slices. Reassemble oranges, spearing each with a wooden pick through center if necessary. Place in a serving dish; spoon syrup over. Sprinkle with chilled orange peel. Makes 8 servings, 2 oranges each.

Clockwise from top: Mince Tarts, page 11; Potatoes in Cream Sauce; Winter Salad; Caramelized Oranges; Old-Fashioned Meat Pie

Supper for 10

Carrot & Coriander Soup*
Herbed Bread*
Curried-Turkey Salad with Rice*
Tomato, Bean & Artichoke Salad*
Rum Syllabub with Brandy
Snaps*
Ginger Gâteau*

*Recipe included in book

# Herbed Bread

| | |
|---|---|
| 1 large French-bread loaf | 1 garlic clove, crushed |
| 3/4 cup butter or margarine, room temperature | 2 tablespoons Italian seasoning |
| | Freshly ground pepper |

**1.** Preheat oven to 400F (205C). Cut loaf diagonally into 1-inch-thick slices without cutting through bottom crust.
**2.** In a small bowl, beat butter or margarine until creamy. Beat in garlic, Italian seasoning and pepper.
**3.** Spread seasoned butter or margarine on both sides of each slice of bread. Wrap loaf in foil; place on a baking sheet.
**4.** Bake in preheated oven 10 to 15 minutes or until hot. Slice completely through; serve hot. Makes 10 servings.

# Carrot & Coriander Soup

| | |
|---|---|
| 6 tablespoons butter or margarine | Freshly ground pepper |
| 2 medium onions, chopped | 1 tablespoon ground coriander |
| 1-1/2 lb. carrots, sliced | 1 bay leaf |
| 3 tablespoons all-purpose flour | 1 tablespoon lemon juice |
| 4 cups chicken stock | 2 cups milk |
| Salt | 1/2 cup half and half |

**1.** Melt butter or margarine in a large saucepan over low heat. Add onions; sauté 5 minutes or until soft and lightly browned. Stir in carrots; cook 3 minutes.
**2.** Stir in flour; cook 1 minute. Gradually stir in stock; bring to a boil.
**3.** Season with salt and pepper. Stir in coriander, bay leaf and lemon juice. Cover pan; simmer about 30 minutes or until carrots are tender.
**4.** Discard bay leaf. In a blender or food processor fitted with a steel blade, process soup until smooth.
**5.** Pour into rinsed saucepan; stir in milk. Bring almost to a boil. Stir in half and half; heat through. Serve immediately in warmed soup bowls. Serve with Herbed Bread, above right. Makes 10 servings.

# Curried-Turkey Salad with Rice

| | |
|---|---|
| 2-1/2 cups uncooked long-grain white rice | 2 to 2-1/2 lb. cooked turkey meat, cubed |
| Salt | 1 (15-oz.) can pineapple chunks, drained |
| 5 cups water | 1 bunch green onions, chopped |
| 3 tablespoons chopped fresh parsley | 2 cups cooked green peas |
| Grated peel of 1 lemon | 8 to 10 celery stalks, sliced |
| 1 cup mayonnaise | |
| 6 tablespoons French dressing | *To garnish:* |
| 1-1/2 to 2 teaspoons curry powder | Radish sprouts |
| Freshly ground pepper | |
| 1 lb. garlic bologna, thinly sliced | |

**1.** In a large saucepan, cook rice in salted water 15 to 20 minutes or until tender and all water has been absorbed. Stir in parsley and lemon peel. Cover and refrigerate until chilled.
**2.** In a large bowl, combine mayonnaise, French dressing and curry powder. Season with salt and pepper.
**3.** Reserve 12 bologna slices. Chop remaining bologna. Stir chopped sausage and turkey into dressing until coated. Stir in pineapple, onions, peas and celery. Cover and refrigerate until chilled.
**4.** Arrange chilled rice around edge of a large serving dish; spoon turkey mixture into center.
**5.** Roll reserved bologna into cornets; arrange around edge of salad on rice. Garnish with radish sprouts. Makes 10 servings.

# Tomato, Bean & Artichoke Salad

1-1/2 lb. green beans, cut
    into 2-inch lengths
Salt
4 (8-oz.) jars marinated
    artichoke hearts,
    drained

1/2 cup French dressing
Freshly ground pepper
5 or 6 small tomatoes,
    quartered

**1.** In a large saucepan of boiling salted water, cook beans 5 minutes or until crisp-tender. Drain; rinse under cold running water. Place cooled beans in a serving bowl.

**2.** Cut artichoke hearts into quarters; add quartered artichokes, dressing, salt and pepper to beans. Toss gently to coat with dressing. Arrange tomato wedges around edge of dish.

**3.** Cover and refrigerate up to 4 hours. Makes 10 servings.

Clockwise from bottom left: Curried-Turkey Salad with Rice, Herbed Bread, Carrot & Coriander Soup, Tomato, Bean & Artichoke Salad

# Ginger Gâteau

*Cake:*
4 eggs
1/2 cup granulated sugar
3/4 cup all-purpose flour
1 teaspoon ground ginger
2 tablespoons butter or
  margarine, melted,
  cooled
Powdered sugar

*Filling:*
1-1/2 cups whipping
  cream
2 tablespoons powdered
  sugar
5 to 6 tablespoons ginger
  marmalade or orange
  marmalade
1 (11-oz.) can
  mandarin-orange
  sections, drained

**1.** Preheat oven to 375F (190C). Grease a 13" x 9" baking pan. Line bottom and sides of pan with waxed paper; grease paper.
**2.** Place eggs and granulated sugar in a large bowl set over a pan of simmering water; beat with an electric mixer until mixture is thick and lemon-colored. Mixture should fall in ribbons when beaters are lifted. Remove bowl from heat; beat until mixture is cool.
**3.** Gradually sift flour and ginger over egg mixture; fold in. Fold in melted butter or margarine until no streaks remain. Spread mixture evenly in prepared pan; smooth top.
**4.** Bake in preheated oven 18 to 20 minutes or until center springs back when lightly pressed.
**5.** Sprinkle a clean towel with powdered sugar. Invert cake onto sugared towel; remove pan. Peel off lining paper; trim crusty edges of cake. Starting from a short end, roll up cake in towel, jelly-roll style. Cool completely on a wire rack.
**6.** To make filling, in a medium bowl, beat cream until soft peaks form. Beat in powdered sugar. Spoon 1 cup whipped-cream mixture into a pastry bag fitted with an open-star tip; set aside. Fold marmalade into remaining whipped-cream mixture.
**7.** Unroll cake; spread with marmalade mixture to within 1/4 inch of edges. Set aside 8 orange sections for decoration. Arrange remaining orange sections over marmalade mixture. Reroll cake, without towel; place, seam-side down, on a serving plate.
**8.** Sift powdered sugar over cake. Pipe reserved whipped cream decoratively down center of cake. Decorate with reserved orange sections. Refrigerate until served. Makes 8 to 10 servings.

# Brandy Snaps

1/4 cup butter or
  margarine
1/4 cup sugar
3 tablespoons light corn
  syrup

1/3 cup all-purpose flour
1/4 teaspoon ground
  ginger

**1.** Preheat oven to 325F (165C). Line baking sheets with parchment paper.
**2.** Melt butter or margarine, sugar and corn syrup in a small saucepan over low heat. Cool slightly.
**3.** Sift flour and ginger over butter mixture; beat with a wooden spoon until blended.
**4.** Drop mixture, 1 teaspoon at a time about 4 inches apart, onto lined baking sheets. Spread to 3-inch circles with a spatula.
**5.** Bake, 1 sheet at a time, in preheated oven 8 to 10 minutes or until golden brown. Cool on baking sheets 1 minute. Remove 1 cookie from paper with a wide flat spatula; wrap cookie around handle of a wooden spoon. Repeat with remaining cookies. Let cool; slide cookies off spoon handles. If cookies become too hard to wrap around spoon, return to oven 1 minute or until pliable. Makes 12 cookies.

# Rum Syllabub

1/2 cup medium-dry
  white wine
Finely grated peel of
  1 orange
1/4 cup sugar

4 to 5 tablespoons rum or
  orange-flavored liqueur
1 pint whipping cream
  (2 cups)

**1.** In a large bowl, combine wine, orange peel and sugar. Cover and let stand about 1 hour.
**2.** Stir in rum or liqueur; pour in cream. Beat until soft peaks form.
**3.** Pour into 10 small wine glasses. Refrigerate up to 30 minutes. Serve with Brandy Snaps, above. Makes 10 servings.

Top to bottom: Rum Syllabub, Brandy Snaps, Ginger Gâteau

## New Year's Eve

Smoked-Fish & Olive Pâté*
Cocktail Rounds or Crackers
Bean-Sprout Salad*
Apple-Cabbage Salad*
Lasagna*
Mocha-Filled
Cream Puffs*
Lemon & Lime Soufflé*
Cheese & Fruit Tray

*Recipe included in book

This is an attractive assortment of supper dishes for a traditional New Year's Eve party. The cream puffs and soufflé can be made ahead and frozen.

## Bean-Sprout Salad

4 oz. fresh mushrooms,
  thinly sliced
1 cup French dressing
2 lb. fresh bean sprouts
  (about 8 cups)

4 carrots, julienned
2 cups thinly shredded
  red cabbage
3 cartons radish sprouts
  or alfalfa sprouts

**1.** Place mushrooms in a large salad bowl; stir in French dressing. Let stand 30 minutes.
**2.** Add remaining ingredients; toss to combine. Serve immediately. Makes 20 servings.

Clockwise from top right: Lasagna, Bean-Sprout Salad, Smoked-Fish & Olive Pâté, Whole-wheat rolls, Apple-Cabbage Salad

# Lasagna

1 tablespoon vegetable oil
Salt
1 lb. green lasagna
noodles

*Meat Sauce:*
1-1/2 lb. lean ground beef
2 lb. lean ground pork
8 oz. chicken livers,
finely chopped
2 onions, finely chopped
2 garlic cloves, crushed
1-1/4 cups finely
chopped carrots
1/4 cup tomato paste
2 (1-lb.) cans tomatoes
1-1/2 cups tomato juice
2 tablespoons
Worcestershire sauce

1/2 teaspoon ground
nutmeg
8 oz. mushrooms, if
desired, chopped
Freshly ground pepper

*White Sauce:*
1/2 cup butter or
margarine
1/2 cup all-purpose flour
1 qt. milk (4 cups)
2 teaspoons dry mustard
2 cups shredded
mozzarella cheese
(8 oz.)

1. Add 1 tablespoon oil to a large saucepan of boiling salted water. Add noodles, 3 or 4 at a time; cook according to package directions until tender. Drain; rinse with cold water. Lay out flat. Repeat with remaining noodles.
2. To make meat sauce, in a large heavy saucepan over medium heat, cook beef and pork, without added fat, until browned. Stir to break up meat. Stir in chicken livers, onions, garlic and carrots; cook about 10 minutes, stirring frequently. Drain off excess fat.
3. Stir in tomato paste, tomatoes, tomato juice, Worcestershire sauce, nutmeg and mushrooms, if desired. Season with salt and pepper. Bring to a boil; reduce heat. Cover and simmer 30 minutes, stirring occasionally.
4. To make white sauce, melt butter or margarine in a medium saucepan over medium heat. Stir in flour; cook 1 minute, stirring. Gradually stir in milk; bring to a boil, stirring. Reduce heat; simmer 2 minutes. Season with salt and pepper. Stir in mustard and 1/2 of cheese. Stir until cheese melts.
5. Preheat oven to 400F (205C). Grease 2 (13" x 9") baking dishes. Alternate layers of noodles, meat sauce and white sauce, ending with white sauce. Sprinkle with remaining cheese.
6. Bake in preheated oven 40 to 50 minutes or until hot and bubbly. Serve hot. Makes 20 servings.

# Smoked-Fish & Olive Pâté

1 onion, chopped
4 hard-cooked eggs,
chopped
12 pimento-stuffed green
olives, sliced
1-1/2 lb. smoked
whitefish, chopped
Freshly ground pepper
1 to 2 garlic cloves,
crushed

3/4 cup plain yogurt

*To garnish:*
2 tablespoons chopped
fresh parsley
16 pimento-stuffed green
olives, sliced

1. In a blender or food processor fitted with a steel blade, process onion and eggs until finely chopped. Add olives and whitefish; process until smooth.
2. Season with pepper. Add garlic and yogurt; process until smooth.
3. Stir in more yogurt if too thick to spread.
4. Spoon pâté into 2 serving dishes; sprinkle with chopped parsley. Arrange sliced olives around edge. Serve with cocktail rounds or crackers. Makes 20 servings.

# Apple-Cabbage Salad

2 green-skinned apples,
cored, thinly sliced
2 tablespoons lemon juice
2 heads Chinese cabbage,
finely sliced
1 cucumber, diced
2 green peppers, thinly
sliced

1 bunch green onions,
chopped
1 bunch celery, thinly
sliced
2 bunches watercress,
coarsely chopped
1 cup French dressing

1. In a large salad bowl, toss apples with lemon juice.
2. Add all remaining ingredients except dressing. Cover and refrigerate up to 8 hours.
3. Pour French dressing over salad; toss to coat with dressing. Serve immediately. Makes 20 servings.

## Mocha-Filled Cream Puffs

2 recipes Cream Puffs,
  page 16

*Filling:*
2 qts. mocha ice cream,
  softened

*Easy Chocolate Sauce:*
6 tablespoons unsweetned
  cocoa powder
3/4 cup corn syrup

3/4 cup butter or
  margarine
1-1/2 cups half and half
2 teaspoons vanilla

**1.** Make and bake Cream Puffs, as directed on page 16. Cool completely on a wire rack.
**2.** Fill each cream puff with about 3 tablespoons ice cream. If making ahead, place in freezer until about 15 minutes before serving.
**3.** To make sauce, in a medium saucepan over low heat, combine all ingredients. Cook, stirring constantly, until smooth. Boil 3 minutes or until slightly reduced. Serve hot or refrigerate until chilled.
**4.** To serve, arrange filled cream puffs in a serving dish. Spoon a little chocolate sauce over each cream puff. Serve remaining sauce separately. Makes about 48 cream puffs.

## Lemon & Lime Soufflé

2 (1/4-oz.) envelopes
  unflavored gelatin
  (2 tablespoons)
1/2 cup water
Grated peel and juice of
  3 lemons
Grated peel and juice of
  2 limes
8 eggs, separated

1-1/2 cups superfine
  sugar
1-3/4 cups whipping
  cream

*To decorate:*
Kiwifruit slices
Lime slices

**1.** In a small saucepan, combine gelatin and water. Stir well; let stand 3 minutes. Stir over low heat until gelatin dissolves; set aside to cool.
**2.** Reserve lemon peel and lime peel. In a large bowl, beat lemon juice, lime juice, egg yolks and 1 cup sugar until foamy. Place bowl over pan of simmering water; cook, beating constantly, until mixture thickens and coats back of a spoon. Remove bowl from water; stir in gelatin mixture. Add reserved lemon peel and lime peel; stir until combined. Refrigerate until mixture mounds when dropped from a spoon.
**3.** Cut a piece of foil large enough to wrap around outside of a 2-quart soufflé dish and extend 2 to 3 inches above rim of dish. Secure foil to dish with kitchen string or tape.
**4.** In a medium bowl, beat cream until soft peaks form. Fold whipped cream into lemon-lime mixture. In a medium bowl, beat egg whites until stiff but not dry. Gradually beat in remaining 1/2 cup sugar; beat until stiff and glossy. Fold beaten egg whites into lemon-lime mixture. Pour mixture into prepared dish; smooth top. Refrigerate several hours or until set. Carefully remove foil collar; decorate soufflé with kiwifruit slices and lime slices. Makes 18 to 20 servings.

Left to right: Mocha-Filled Cream Puffs, Lemon & Lime Soufflé

### New Year's Day Open House

Sausage & Shrimp Bacon Rolls*
Curry Puffs with Watercress Dip*
Cheese Dip*    Cheese Sables*
Cheese Twists*    Cocktail Canapés*
Celery & Peanut Boats*
Chicken Pinwheels*
Olive & Ham Rolls*
White-Wine Cup*
Mulled Wine*

*Recipe included in book

## Mulled Wine

3 (750ml.) bottles burgundy
    or other red wine
1/2 cup brandy
1 cup raisins
3/4 cup sugar

10 whole cloves
1 teaspoon cardamom
    seeds, if desired
1 (3-inch) cinnamon stick
Thin peel of 2 lemons

1. In a large saucepan over low heat, combine all ingredients. Stir until sugar dissolves.
2. Simmer 30 minutes. Remove and discard cloves, cinnamon, cardamom and lemon peel. Makes 20 (1/2-cup) servings.

## Cheese Sables

1-1/4 cups sifted
    all-purpose flour
1/2 teaspoon salt
1/8 teaspoon pepper
1/8 teaspoon red
    (cayenne) pepper
3/4 cup shredded
    Cheddar cheese (3 oz.)
1/4 cup grated Parmesan
    cheese

1/2 cup butter or
    margarine
1 egg yolk, beaten
3 tablespoons iced water
About 3 tablespoons milk
2 tablespoons finely
    chopped walnuts or
    pecans

1. In a medium bowl, combine flour, salt, pepper and cayenne. Stir in cheeses until blended. With a pastry blender or 2 knives, cut in butter or margarine until mixture resembles coarse crumbs. Sprinkle with egg yolk and iced water; toss with a fork until mixture binds together. Knead dough in bowl 8 to 10 strokes or until smooth.
2. Divide dough in half. Shape each piece into a 7 x 1-1/4-inch roll. Wrap separately; refrigerate 1 hour.
3. Preheat oven to 375F (190C). Line baking sheets with parchment paper.
4. Cut rolls into 1/4-inch-thick slices. Place slices, cut-side down, about 1 inch apart on lined baking sheets. Brush tops with milk; sprinkle with chopped nuts.
5. Bake in preheated oven 10 to 12 minutes or until golden. Remove from baking sheets; cool completely on wire racks. Makes 56 pastries.

## Cheese Dip

1/2 cup crumbled blue
    cheese (6 oz.), room
    temperature
1 small onion, finely
    chopped
2 celery stalks, chopped
1 hard-cooked egg,
    chopped
Salt

1 teaspoon paprika
1 teaspoon sugar
1 tablespoon lemon juice
1 tablespoon white-wine
    vinegar
About 1/4 cup milk

*To serve:*
Crudités

1. In a blender or food processor fitted with a steel blade, process cheese, onion. celery and egg until smooth. Add remaining ingredients; process again until smooth. Add additional milk if necessary to give a good consistency for dipping.
2. Serve with crudités, such as celery sticks, sliced carrots, bell-pepper strips, green onions and raw cauliflowerets. Makes about 2 cups.

# Celery & Peanut Boats

1/4 cup crunchy peanut
  butter
2 tablespoons butter or
  margarine, room
  temperature
Salt
Freshly ground pepper
1 tablespoon finely
  chopped green-onion
  tops or chives

Pinch of dried leaf thyme
Pinch of garlic salt,
  if desired
1/4 cup fresh bread
  crumbs
A few drops of lemon
  juice
6 celery stalks, trimmed

**1.** In a small bowl, beat peanut butter and butter or marga-rine until smooth. Season with salt and pepper. Stir in onion tops or chives, thyme and garlic salt, if desired. Stir in bread crumbs; stir in enough lemon juice to give a good consistency for spreading.
**2.** Spoon mixture into celery stalks.
**3.** Cut filled celery into 1-inch lengths. Arrange on a plate. Cover and refrigerate until served. Makes about 40 appetizers.

# Sausage & Shrimp Bacon Rolls

20 bacon slices
20 cocktail sausages

20 cooked, deveined,
  peeled shrimp

**1.** Preheat broiler. Lay bacon slices on a flat surface; stretch slightly with back of a knife. Cut each piece in half crosswise.
**2.** Wrap a half slice of bacon around each sausage; wrap remaining bacon around shrimp. Secure with wooden picks.
**3.** Cook under preheated broiler 4 or 5 inches from heat 5 to 10 minutes, turning once, until bacon is crisp. Serve hot. Makes 40 appetizers.

Clockwise from left: Cheese Dip, Cheese Sables, Crudités, Mulled Wine, Celery & Peanut Boats, Sausage & Shrimp Bacon Rolls

# White-Wine Cup

| | |
|---|---|
| 4 (750ml.) bottles dry white wine, chilled | 1 orange, thinly sliced |
| 4 to 6 tablespoons orange-flavored liqueur | 1 apple, cored, sliced |
| 1/4 medium cucumber, thinly sliced | *To serve:* |
| | Crushed ice |
| | 1 qt. soda water, chilled |

1. Combine wine, liqueur, cucumber, orange and apple in a large bowl. Refrigerate until chilled.
2. To serve, put crushed ice in a punch bowl or large pitcher. Add chilled wine mixture and soda water. Serve immediately. Makes about 30 (1/2-cup) servings.

# Cheese Twists

| | |
|---|---|
| 1/2 (17-1/2-oz.) pkg. frozen puff pastry, thawed | 3 tablespoons grated Parmesan cheese |
| About 3 tablespoons milk | |

1. Preheat oven to 425F (220C). Grease 2 baking sheets. On a lightly floured surface, roll out pastry to a 12-inch square about 1/8-inch thick. Trim edges neatly with a sharp knife. Cut pastry into quarters; cut each quarter into 1/2- to 3/4-inch-wide strips.
2. Brush strips with milk. Sprinkle with cheese. Give each strip 1 or 2 twists. Place on greased baking sheets.
3. Bake in preheated oven about 12 minutes or until lightly browned. Remove from baking sheet; cool on wire racks. Serve warm or cold. Store in an airtight container. Makes about 36 twists.

# Chicken Pinwheels

| | |
|---|---|
| 1 cup finely chopped cooked chicken | 1 tablespoon chopped fresh parsley, if desired |
| 1 (8-1/2-oz.) can water chestnuts, drained, finely chopped | 1 unsliced whole-wheat-bread loaf, crust removed |
| 2 tablespoons finely chopped onion | |
| Freshly ground pepper | *To garnish:* |
| | Parsley sprigs |

1. In a medium bowl, combine all ingredients except bread.
2. Cut loaf lengthwise into 4 equal slices.
3. Spread bread slices with chicken mixture, spreading mixture almost to edges. Starting with a long side, roll up each slice, jelly-roll style. Wrap rolls tightly in plastic wrap. Refrigerate at least 1 hour or overnight.
4. Cut rolls crosswise into thin slices. Arrange on a plate. Garnish with parsley sprigs. Makes about 45 pinwheels.

**Variation**
**Olive & Ham Rolls:** Spread bread with 1/2 cup room-temperature butter or margarine. Arrange 1/2 pound thinly-sliced ham over butter or margarine. Place a roll of pimento-stuffed green olives along 1 long edge of each bread slice. Starting from edge with olives, roll up, jelly-roll style. Finish as directed above.

# Cocktail Canapés

| | |
|---|---|
| 1/4 cucumber, sliced | 1 (4-oz.) carton whipped cream cheese, room temperature |
| 24 small crackers | |
| 4 hard-cooked eggs | |
| 4 oz. deveined, peeled, cooked medium shrimp | 2 oz. smoked-salmon pieces |
| Fresh parsley sprigs | 12 cooked asparagus tips |

1. Cut cucumber slices in half. On each of 12 crackers, place a hard-cooked-egg slice, half a cucumber slice, a shrimp and a parsley sprig.
2. Roll salmon into 12 small rolls. On each of 12 remaining crackers, place a small smoked-salmon roll in center. Spoon cream cheese into a pastry bag fitted with a star tip. Pipe a row of cream cheese on each side of salmon. Top with an asparagus spear. Makes 24 appetizers.

# Curry Puffs with Watercress Dip

**1/2 recipe Choux Paste, page 16**
**2 tablespoons butter or margarine**
**1 onion, finely chopped**
**2 teaspoons curry powder**
**Vegetable oil for deep-frying**

**Watercress Dip:**
**1/4 cup mayonnaise**
**2 tablespoons plain yogurt**
**1 bunch watercress, finely chopped**
**Grated peel of 1/2 lemon**

**1.** Make Choux Paste as directed on page 16 through step 3. Melt butter or margarine in a small saucepan over low heat. Add onion; sauté about 7 minutes or until lightly browned. Stir in curry powder; cool slightly. Beat curry mixture into choux paste.
**2.** In a large saucepan, heat oil to 375F (190C) or until a 1-inch bread cube turns golden brown in 50 seconds.
**3.** Drop small teaspoons of choux mixture into oil, about 6 at a time. Fry 3 to 4 minutes, turning if necessary, until puffed and golden brown. Drain on paper towels; keep warm. Repeat with remaining dough.
**4.** To make dip, in a small bowl, combine dip ingredients. Garnish with a sprig of watercress, if desired. Place bowl containing watercress dip on a large plate; surround with warm puffs. Makes about 25 puffs.

Clockwise from upper left: White-Wine Cup, Curry Puffs with Watercress Dip, Olive & Ham Rolls, Chicken Pinwheels, Cocktail Canapés, Cheese Twists

Twelfth Night

Goat Cheese with Pears*
Paupiettes of Sole Bon Noël*
Buttered Green Noodles
Tossed Salad
Raspberry Trifle*

*Recipe included in book

## Paupiettes of Sole Bon Noël

6 (8- to 10-oz.) sole fillets,
 skinned
Salt
Freshly ground pepper
1 (14-oz.) can asparagus
 spears, drained
6 oz. deveined, peeled
 uncooked shrimp
3 tablespoons butter or
 margarine

1 cup dry white wine
1 tablespoon cornstarch
1/2 cup dairy sour cream
1 egg yolk
3 tablespoons dry bread
 crumbs

*To garnish:*
6 unpeeled cooked shrimp

**1.** Preheat oven to 375F (190C). Grease a 13" x 9" baking dish. Lay sole fillets on a flat surface, skinned-side up; season with salt and pepper.
**2.** Divide asparagus spears among sole fillets. Arrange 3/4 of shrimp over asparagus. Roll up fillets. Place rolls, seam-side down, in greased baking dish.
**3.** Scatter remaining shrimp over rolls; dot with butter or margarine. Add wine to dish. Cover with foil.
**4.** Bake in preheated oven about 25 minutes or until sole is done. Sole is done when it is opaque when a fork is inserted into thickest portion.
**5.** Preheat broiler. Place sole on a heatproof serving dish; keep warm. Drain cooking liquid into a saucepan. In a small bowl, blend cornstarch, sour cream and egg yolk; whisk mixture into cooking liquid. Bring to a boil, stirring constantly. Reduce heat; simmer 2 minutes. Season with salt and pepper. Pour sauce over sole.
**6.** Sprinkle sole with bread crumbs. Cook under preheated broiler until lightly browned. Garnish with whole shrimp; serve immediately. Makes 6 servings.

## Goat Cheese with Pears

12 oz. goat cheese
3 ripe pears
Juice of 1 lemon
1 bunch watercress,
 trimmed
18 walnut halves

*To serve:*
Hot whole-wheat toast or
 crackers

**1.** Cut goat cheese into 12 equal slices. Set aside.
**2.** Peel and core pears. Slice each pear into 8 slices. In a medium bowl, combine pears and lemon juice; toss to coat. Drain off excess juice.
**3.** Arrange 4 pear slices on each of 6 small plates. Add 2 slices of cheese to each plate. Garnish with watercress and walnut halves. Serve with hot whole-wheat toast or crackers. Makes 6 servings.

# Raspberry Trifle

1 (8-inch) sponge cake
3/4 cup raspberry jam
1/4 cup sherry
1 (10-oz.) pkg. frozen
    raspberries, partly
    thawed

*Custard:*
2 tablespoons cornstarch
1/4 cup sugar

2 cups milk
4 egg yolks
1 teaspoon vanilla extract

*Topping:*
1/2 pint whipping cream
    (1 cup)
Walnut halves
Angelica

**1.** Split cake in half horizontally; spread bottom half with jam. Reassemble cake. Cut into 1-inch cubes; place in a glass serving bowl. Sprinkle with sherry.
**2.** Arrange raspberries over cake; let stand until completely thawed so juices are absorbed by cake.
**3.** To make custard, in a medium saucepan, combine cornstarch and sugar. Gradually whisk in milk and egg yolks. Cook over medium heat, stirring, until mixture boils and is thickened. Stir in vanilla. Cool slightly. Pour cooled custard over raspberries. Refrigerate until chilled.
**4.** In a medium bowl, beat cream until soft peaks form. Spoon into a pastry bag fitted with a large star tip. Pipe a design like spokes of a wheel on top of trifle. Decorate with walnuts and angelica; refrigerate until served. Makes 6 to 8 servings.

Left to right: Paupiettes of Sole Bon Noël, Raspberry Trifle, Goat Cheese with Pears, Toast

# Turkey Leftovers

## Turkey Soup

1 turkey carcass
1 onion, quartered
4 carrots, halved
1 bay leaf
8 cups water
2 onions, finely chopped
2 leeks, finely chopped
2 parsnips, finely chopped
2 celery stalks, finely
   chopped
1 tablespoon
   Worcestershire sauce

1/4 cup uncooked
   long-grain white rice
Salt
Freshly ground pepper
1/3 cup all-purpose flour
1/4 cup butter or
   margarine
1/2 cup half and half,
   if desired

1. Break up carcass. In a large pot, combine carcass, onion, carrots, bay leaf and water. Bring to a boil. Reduce heat. Cover and simmer 1 hour. Skim surface as necessary. Or, cook in a pressure cooker 15 minutes.
2. Strain stock; discard onion and bay leaf. Remove any meat from bones; chop cooked carrots.
3. In a clean saucepan, combine strained stock, turkey from bones, chopped carrots, remaining vegetables, Worcestershire sauce and rice. Season with salt and pepper. Bring to a boil. Reduce heat; cover. Simmer 30 minutes, stirring occasionally.
4. In a small bowl, combine flour and butter or margarine. Whisk 1 cup of hot soup into flour mixture. Add to soup, stirring until blended. Cook 5 minutes. Stir in half and half, if desired. Serve soup in warmed soup bowls. Makes 10 to 12 servings.

**Variation**
For a thick smooth soup, puree, in batches, in a blender or food processor fitted with a steel blade.

## Turkey, Ham & Almond Pie

3 tablespoons butter or
   margarine
1/4 cup sliced almonds
3 tablespoons all-purpose
   flour
1/2 cup dry white wine
1 cup chicken stock or
   milk
Salt
Freshly ground pepper
1-1/2 teaspoons dried
   leaf marjoram or dried
   leaf oregano

2 tablespoons dairy sour
   cream or mayonnaise
1/2 cup seedless green
   grapes, halved
1-1/2 cups diced cooked
   turkey
1/2 cup diced ham
2 recipes Shortcrust
   Pastry, page 16
About 3 tablespoons milk

1. Melt butter or margarine in a medium skillet over medium heat. Add almonds; sauté until lightly browned. Stir in flour; cook 1 minute, stirring. Gradually stir in wine and stock or milk; cook, stirring constantly, until mixture thickens and comes to a boil. Season with salt and pepper; stir in marjoram or oregano. Cool slightly. Stir in sour cream or mayonnaise, grapes, turkey and ham.
2. Prepare pastry as directed on page 16.
3. Preheat oven to 425F (220C). Divide pastry in half. On a lightly floured surface, roll out 1/2 of pastry to an 11-inch circle. Use pastry to line a 9-inch pie pan. Spoon in filling.
4. Roll out remaining pastry to a 10-inch circle. Place over filling. Trim edges even with rim of pan. Press to seal. Crimp edge. Make a hole in center of pie. Brush pastry with milk.
5. Bake in preheated oven 20 minutes. Reduce oven temperature to 350F (175C); bake 20 to 30 minutes or until pastry is golden brown. Serve hot or cold. Makes 4 or 5 servings.

# Easy Turkey & Broccoli Casserole

1 (10-oz.) pkg. frozen
   broccoli spears
8 thick slices cooked
   turkey
1 (10-3/4-oz.) can
   condensed cream of
   chicken soup
2 tablespoons lemon juice

2 to 3 tablespoons dry
   white wine
1/4 cup mayonnaise
Freshly ground pepper
1/2 cup fresh bread
   crumbs
1/4 cup shredded
   Cheddar cheese (1 oz.)

**1.** Preheat oven to 425F (220C). Grease a shallow baking dish. Cook broccoli in boiling salted water according to package directions. Drain; arrange in greased dish.
**2.** Arrange turkey slices over broccoli.
**3.** In a medium bowl, combine soup, lemon juice, wine and mayonnaise. Season well with pepper. Spoon mixture over turkey.
**4.** In a small bowl, combine bread crumbs and cheese; sprinkle over soup mixture.
**5.** Bake in preheated oven 25 to 30 minutes or until bubbling and golden brown. Serve hot. Makes 4 servings.

Left to right: Easy Turkey & Broccoli Casserole, Turkey Soup

# Deep Turkey Pie

**Pastry:**
3-1/2 cups all-purpose
  flour
1 teaspoon salt
1 cup vegetable
  shortening
1/4 cup water
1/4 cup milk

**Filling:**
8 oz. lean ground pork
1 small onion
2 cups chopped cooked
  ham
1/2 teaspoon ground
  coriander
Freshly ground pepper
3 cups chopped cooked
  turkey
1 egg, beaten

**1.** In a medium bowl, combine flour and salt. With a pastry blender or 2 knives, cut in shortening until mixture resembles coarse crumbs.

**2.** Add water and milk; toss with a fork until mixture binds together. Knead in bowl 8 to 10 strokes or until smooth. Shape pastry into a flattened ball. Wrap and refrigerate while preparing filling.

**3.** Preheat oven to 400F (205C). To prepare filling, in a medium skillet over medium heat, cook pork and onion without any added fat. Cook, stirring, until pork is no longer pink. Drain excess fat. Spoon cooked mixture into a medium bowl; stir in ham and coriander. Season with pepper. Set aside.

**4.** Divide dough into 2 pieces, making 1 piece 2/3 of dough. On a lightly floured surface, roll out large piece of dough into a piece large enough to line a pâté mold, 7- to 8-inches around or a 9" x 5" loaf pan. Use pastry to line bottom and sides of pan.

**5.** Spoon 1/2 of pork mixture into pastry-lined pan; cover with chopped turkey. Spoon remaining pork mixture over turkey. Press down.

**6.** Roll out remaining pastry into a piece slightly larger than top of pan, reserving pastry trimmings. Press edges to seal. Trim edges and flute. Make a hole in center. Brush with beaten egg.

**7.** Roll out pastry trimmings; cut out leaves. Place leaves around central hole; brush leaves with beaten egg.

**8.** Bake in preheated oven 30 minutes. Reduce oven temperature to 325F (160C); bake 20 to 30 minutes or until pastry is golden brown.

**9.** Place on a wire rack, cool slightly. Serve warm or refrigerate until served. Cut into slices to serve. Makes 8 servings.

# Turkey & Spinach Crepes

**Crepes:**
1/2 cup all-purpose flour,
  sifted
1/4 teaspoon salt
2 eggs
2/3 cup milk
2 tablespoons butter or
  margarine, melted

**Filling:**
1/4 cup butter or
  margarine
1 medium onion, chopped
2 tablespoons all-purpose
  flour
1-1/4 cups milk or
  chicken broth
Salt
Freshly ground pepper
1/4 teaspoon grated
  nutmeg

1 (10-oz.) pkg. frozen
  chopped spinach,
  cooked, drained
2 cups diced cooked
  turkey
3 tablespoons finely
  chopped walnuts

**Sauce:**
3 tablespoons butter or
  margarine
3 tablespoons all-purpose
  flour
1-1/2 cups milk
1 teaspoon Dijon-style
  mustard
Salt
Freshly ground pepper
1/3 cup shredded
  Cheddar cheese

**1.** To make crepes, in a medium bowl, combine flour and salt. In a small bowl, beat eggs and milk until blended. Add beaten egg mixture to flour; beat with a whisk until thoroughly blended. Add melted butter or margarine; beat well. Or place ingredients in a blender or food processor with a steel blade. Process 1 to 2 minutes or until batter is smooth. Refrigerate 1 hour.

**2.** Melt about 1 teaspoon butter in a 7- or 8-inch crepe pan or skillet over medium heat. Stir crepe batter. Spoon 2 to 3 tablespoons batter into pan, swirling batter to cover bottom of pan. Cook 1-1/2 minutes. Turn crepe; cook 1-1/2 minutes. Slide cooked crepe onto a flat dish; repeat with remaining batter to make 8 crepes. Set aside.

**3.** Preheat oven to 425F (220C). Grease a shallow baking dish. To make filling, melt butter or margarine in medium skillet. Add onion; sauté until transparent. Stir in flour; cook 1 minute, stirring. Gradually stir in milk or chicken broth; cook, stirring constantly, until mixture thickens and comes to a boil. Season with salt, pepper and nutmeg. Stir in spinach, turkey and walnuts.

**4.** Spoon about 3 tablespoons turkey mixture onto center of each crepe. Roll or fold crepe; place in a single layer, seam-side down, in greased baking dish.

**5.** To make sauce, melt butter or margarine in a medium saucepan. Stir in flour; cook 1 minute. Gradually stir in milk; cook, stirring constantly, until mixture thickens and comes to a boil. Stir in mustard. Remove pan from heat. Season with salt and pepper. Pour sauce over filled crepes; sprinkle with cheese.

**6.** Bake in preheated oven 15 to 20 minutes or until top is lightly browned. Serve immediately. Makes 4 servings.

# Turkey Sandwich Spread

2 cups ground cooked
   turkey
1 onion, finely chopped
1 to 2 garlic cloves,
   crushed
1/2 cup finely chopped
   sweet pickles

1 tablespoon sherry or
   port
1/2 cup mayonnaise
Salt
Freshly ground pepper

**1.** In a medium bowl, combine turkey, onion, garlic, pickles, sherry or port and mayonnaise. Season with salt and pepper.
**2.** Refrigerate until chilled. Makes about 3 cups.

Top to bottom: Deep Turkey Pie, Turkey & Spinach Crepes

### Romantic Christmas

Smoked-Salmon & Shrimp Salad*
Cranberry Duck*
Minty Peas*
Oven-Roasted Potatoes
Apple-Filled Crepes with
Brandy Sauce*

*Recipe included in book

## Smoked-Salmon & Shrimp Salad

| | |
|---|---|
| 3 tablespoons mayonnaise | 1 teaspoon lemon juice |
| 1/2 teaspoon prepared horseradish | 4 oz. cooked, deveined, peeled shrimp |
| 1 teaspoon capers, chopped | 2 smoked-salmon slices (3 to 4 oz. each) |
| 1 teaspoon chopped fresh parsley | Lettuce leaves |
| | Cucumber slices |
| | Lemon slices |

1. In a medium bowl, combine mayonnaise, horseradish, capers, parsley and lemon juice. Stir in shrimp until coated.
2. Lay salmon slices on a flat surface; divide shrimp mixture equally between them. Roll up carefully.
3. Arrange lettuce leaves on 2 small plates; place salmon rolls on lettuce. Garnish with cucumber and lemon slices; serve with whole-wheat toast and butter, if desired. Makes 2 servings.

## Minty Peas

| | |
|---|---|
| 1 (10-oz.) pkg. frozen green peas | 3 tablespoons dairy sour cream |
| Salt | 2 to 4 baked tart shells, above, if desired |
| 1 drop mint flavoring | |

1. Cook peas in boiling salted water according to package directions. Drain well.
2. In a small bowl, stir mint flavoring into sour cream. Top each servings of peas with a little sour-cream mixture. If desired, fill baked tart shells with hot peas; top each tart with a little sour-cream mixture. Makes 2 to 4 servings.

## Cranberry Duck

| | |
|---|---|
| 1 (4- to 5-lb.) duck, oven-ready | Juice of 1 orange |
| Salt | Juice of 1 lemon |
| 1/2 cup beef stock | 1-1/2 teaspoons cornstarch |
| 2 to 3 tablespoons cranberry sauce | Water |
| 2 to 3 tablespoons port or sherry | Freshly ground pepper |
| Grated peel of 1/2 orange | *To garnish:* |
| | Orange wedges |

1. Preheat oven to 425F (220C). Remove and discard excess fat and giblets from duck. Prick skin all over with a fork to allow fat to escape during roasting. Place duck, breast-side up, on a rack in a roasting pan. Sprinkle lightly with salt.
2. Roast in preheated oven about 1-1/2 hours or until duck is done, basting with pan drippings once during cooking. Duck is done when juices run clear when duck is pierced between breast and thigh or a thermometer registers 180F (80C).
3. Transfer duck to a serving dish; keep warm. Remove fat from pan drippings. Stir stock, cranberry sauce, port or sherry, orange peel, orange juice and lemon juice into pan. Bring to a boil, stirring and scraping browned bits from pan into sauce. Simmer 2 to 3 minutes.
4. In a small bowl, blend cornstarch with a little cold water to make a smooth paste. Stir cornstarch mixture into pan; simmer 2 to 3 minutes or until thickened, stirring. Season with salt and pepper. Pour sauce into a warmed sauce dish.
5. Garnish duck with orange wedges. Makes 2 to 4 servings.

## Pastry Shells

**1/2 recipe Shortcrust Pastry, page 16**

1. Preheat oven to 400F (205C). Prepare and chill pastry as directed on page 16. On a lightly floured surface, roll out pastry to 1/4 inch thick. Cut into 3-inch circles. Use circles to line 2-1/2-inch tart pans. Prick pastry with a fork.
2. Bake in preheated oven 10 to 12 minutes or until golden brown. Fill warm tarts with Minty Peas, below, if desired. Makes 6 tarts.

# Apple-Filled Crepes

4 Crepes, from Turkey &
  Spinach Crepes, page 44

*Filling:*
2 small tart apples,
  peeled, cored, sliced
2 to 3 tablespoons apple
  cider or apple juice
About 1/4 cup firmly packed
  light-brown sugar
2 to 3 tablespoons
  prepared mincemeat

1/4 teaspoon ground
  cinnamon

*To serve:*
Brandy Sauce, below
3 tablespoons butter
  or margarine
Orange slices

1. Prepare and cook crepes according to directions on page 44, reserving remaining crepes for another use.
2. In a medium saucepan, combine apples and cider or juice. Bring to a boil over medium heat. Reduce heat; cover and simmer until apples are barely tender. Drain off any excess liquid. Stir in brown sugar to taste, mincemeat and cinnamon. Remove from heat.

3. Spoon 2 to 3 tablespoons apple filling onto center of each crepe. Fold crepe over filling; roll, enclosing filling completely. Refrigerate filled crepes up to 4 hours.
4. To serve, prepare Brandy Sauce; keep warm. Melt butter or margarine in a medium skillet. Add crepes, seam-side down. Cook over medium heat until lightly browned and crisp on all sides. Remove with a slotted spoon; drain on paper towels. Place 2 crepes on each plate. Decorate with orange slices. Serve with Brandy Sauce. Makes 2 servings.

# Brandy Sauce

1 teaspoon cornstarch
1 tablespoon sugar
1/2 cup milk
1 egg yolk

2 tablespoons butter or
  margarine
2 to 3 tablespoons brandy

1. In a medium saucepan, combine cornstarch and sugar. Gradually whisk in milk and egg yolk. Cook over medium heat, stirring, until mixture comes to a boil and is slightly thickened.
2. Stir in butter or margarine and brandy to taste. Serve warm with Apple-Filled Crepes. Makes about 3/4 cup.

Left to right: Smoked-Salmom & Shrimp Salad, Cranberry Duck with Minty-Pea Tarts

*Vegetarian Christmas*

Zucchini Ratatouille*
Pine-Nut Loaf*
Spicy Tomato Sauce*
Buttered Brussel Sprouts &
Mushrooms
Duchess Potatoes*
Mincemeat Tart, page 10

*Recipe included in book

# Duchess Potatoes

| | |
|---|---|
| 3 lb. potatoes, peeled, quartered | Freshly ground pepper |
| Salt | Pinch of grated nutmeg |
| | 1 egg |

**1.** Grease a large baking sheet. Cook potatoes in a large saucepan of boiling salted water about 20 minutes or until tender. Drain well.
**2.** Preheat oven to 350F (175C). Mash potatoes until smooth. Season with salt and pepper. Beat in nutmeg and egg.
**3.** Spoon mixture into a pastry bag fitted with a large star tip. Pipe 12 large whirls of mixture onto greased baking sheet.
**4.** Bake in preheated oven about 25 minutes or until lightly browned. Serve hot. Makes 6 servings.

# Zucchini Ratatouille

| | |
|---|---|
| 1/4 cup olive oil | 1 lb. zucchini, cut in strips |
| 2 large onions, sliced | Salt |
| 1 or 2 garlic cloves, crushed | Freshly ground black pepper |
| 2 red bell peppers, cut in strips | 2 tablespoons white wine |
| 1 green bell pepper, cut in strips | Chopped fresh parsley |

**1.** Heat oil in a medium skillet over low heat. Add onions and garlic to taste; sauté about 5 minutes or until soft and lightly browned. Add bell peppers; cook 3 to 4 minutes or until peppers are soft. Stir in zucchini.
**2.** Season with salt and pepper. Stir in wine; cook about 5 minutes or until zucchini is crisp-tender, stirring occasionally.
**3.** Spoon into a serving dish; sprinkle ratatouille with parsley; serve hot or at room temperature. Makes 6 servings.

# Spicy Tomato Sauce

| | |
|---|---|
| 1 (8-oz.) can tomato sauce | 1 garlic clove, crushed |
| 1 cup red wine | Dash of red (cayenne) pepper |
| Salt | |
| Freshly ground black pepper | |

**1.** In a medium saucepan over medium heat, combine all ingredients. Bring to a boil. Reduce heat; simmer about 10 minutes or until sauce is thick enough to coat back of a spoon.
**2.** Serve with Pine-Nut Loaf. Makes about 1-1/2 cups.

# Pine-Nut Loaf

2 to 3 tablespoons dried
  bread crumbs
2-1/2 tablespoons butter
  or margarine
1 onion, chopped
1/2 cup pine nuts
3/4 cup finely chopped
  cashews
1/2 cup whole almonds,
  ground
2 cups fresh bread crumbs
1/4 cup milk
2 eggs, beaten
Salt
Freshly ground pepper
Freshly grated nutmeg

*Stuffing:*
1/2 cup butter or
  margarine, room
  temperature
Grated peel and juice of
  1/2 lemon
1/2 teaspoon dried leaf
  thyme
1/4 cup chopped fresh
  parsley
1 garlic clove, peeled,
  crushed
2 cups fresh bread crumbs

*To garnish:*
2 tablespoons toasted
  pine nuts
Lemon slices
Parsley sprigs

**1.** Preheat oven to 350F (175C). Line a 9" x 5" loaf pan with waxed paper. Generously butter paper; sprinkle with dried bread crumbs.
**2.** Melt butter or margarine in a medium skillet over low heat. Add onion; sauté about 7 minutes or until soft and lightly browned. Spoon cooked onions into a medium bowl; stir in nuts, fresh bread crumbs, milk, eggs, salt, pepper and nutmeg to taste. Stir until combined.
**3.** To make stuffing, cream butter or margarine in a medium bowl. Gradually stir in remaining ingredients until blended.
**4.** Spoon 1/2 of nut mixture into bottom of prepared pan. Cover with stuffing; add remaining nut mixture. Smooth surface. Grease a piece of foil large enough to cover loaf pan. Cover with piece of greased foil, greased-side down.
**5.** Bake in preheated oven 1 hour. Remove foil; bake 5 to 10 minutes or until browned. Let cool in pan 5 minutes.
**6.** Carefully invert onto a serving dish; gently remove lining paper. Sprinkle toasted pine nuts over top. Garnish with lemon slices and parsley sprigs.
**7.** Serve with Spicy Tomato Sauce or cranberry sauce. Makes 6 servings.

Left to right: Duchess Potatoes, Pine-Nut Loaf, Spicy Tomato Sauce, Zucchini Ratatouille

*Christmas from the Sea*

Grapefruit & Kiwifruit Cups*
Salmon en Croûte*
Buttered Peas & Onions
Hollandaise Sauce*
Soufflé Olivia with Almond Tuiles*

*Recipe included in book

# Almond Tuiles

1 egg white
1/4 cup sugar
1/4 teaspoon almond extract
1/4 cup sifted all-purpose flour

1/4 cup finely ground blanched almonds
2 tablespoons butter or margarine, melted

**1.** Preheat oven to 375F (190C). Line 2 baking sheets with parchment paper.
**2.** In a medium bowl, beat egg white until stiff but not dry. Beat in sugar; beat until stiff and glossy. Fold in almond extract, flour and almonds. Fold in melted butter or margarine until no streaks remain.
**3.** Drop mixture, 1 teaspoon at a time, onto lined baking sheets. Drop mixture about 4 inches apart. Spread to 3-inch circles with a spatula.
**4.** Bake, 1 sheet at a time, in preheated oven 5 to 6 minutes or until edges are golden brown. Cool 1 minute on baking sheet on a wire rack. Carefully remove 1 cookie at a time with a wide flat spatula. Wrap warm cookie around a cream horn form or handle of a wooden spoon. Let cool enough to set shape; slide off form. Repeat with remaining cookies. Makes 12 cookies.

# Salmon en Croûte

2 (12- to 15-oz.) salmon fillets
Juice of 1 lemon
Salt
Freshly ground pepper
1/4 cup butter or margarine, room temperature
1 teaspoon dried dill weed
1 (17-1/2-oz) pkg. frozen puff pastry, thawed
1 egg, beaten

*Hollandaise Sauce:*
6 tablespoons white-wine vinegar

3 tablespoons water
10 peppercorns, crushed
6 egg yolks
3/4 to 1-1/4 cups butter or margarine, cut into pieces
Salt
About 2 teaspoons lemon juice

*To garnish:*
Lemon slices
Cucumber slices
Parsley sprigs

**1.** Preheat oven to 425F (220C). Grease a baking sheet. Rub salmon fillets with lemon juice; season lightly with salt and pepper.
**2.** Lay 1 fillet on a flat surface. Spread with butter or margarine; sprinkle with dill weed. Cover with second fillet.
**3.** Unfold 1 pastry sheet. On a lightly floured surface, roll out unfolded pastry into a rectangle larger than salmon. Place fillets on pastry. Roll out remaining sheet of pastry the same size. Brush pastry around salmon with egg. Place second pastry sheet over salmon. Cut around salmon, making a fish shape. Seal edges.
**4.** Place salmon on greased baking sheet; brush all with egg. Roll out pastry trimmings; cut into narrow strips. Arrange strip over salmon to resemble scales. Make a tail and head, if desired. Brush with beaten egg.
**5.** Bake in preheated oven about 30 minutes. Reduce oven temperature to 375F (190C). Bake 20 minutes or until golden brown. If pastry browns too quickly; cover with a sheet of foil.
**6.** To make Hollandaise Sauce, in a small saucepan, combine vinegar, water and peppercorns. Bring to a boil; boil until reduced by half. Strain into top of a double boiler; beat in egg yolks. Cook over simmering water until thick, stirring constantly. Beat in butter or margarine, a piece at a time, until sauce is smooth. Season with salt and lemon juice. Cover and keep warm.
**7.** Garnish salmon with lemon slices, cucumber slices and parsley sprigs. Serve hot with buttered potatoes, peas and carrots and a salad. Serve Hollandaise Sauce separately. Makes 6 servings.

# Soufflé Olivia

| | |
|---|---|
| 2 tablespoons instant coffee powder | 3 tablespoons milk |
| 1/4 cup boiling water | 2 tablespoons dark rum |
| 4 eggs, separated | 2/3 cup whipping cream |
| 3/4 cup sugar | 4 oz. semisweet chocolate, finely grated |
| 1 (1/4-oz.) envelope unflavored gelatin (1 tablespoon) | 1/3 cup sliced almonds |

1. Dissolve coffee in boiling water; let cool.
2. In a large bowl, beat egg yolks, sugar and cooled coffee about 8 to 10 minutes or until thick.
3. In a small saucepan, combine gelatin and milk. Stir well; let stand 3 minutes. Stir over low heat until gelatin dissolves; cool to room temperature. Add cooled gelatin and rum to coffee mixture; beat until blended.
4. In a medium bowl, beat cream until almost stiff. Fold whipped cream into coffee mixture. Refrigerate 20 minutes.
5. In a medium bowl, beat egg whites until stiff but not dry. Fold beaten egg whites into chilled coffee mixture. In a small bowl, combine grated chocolate and sliced almonds.
6. Spoon 1/3 of coffee mixture into a 1-quart soufflé dish or glass serving bowl. Sprinkle with 1/3 chocolate-almond mixture. Repeat with another 1/3 of coffee mixture and 1/3 of chocolate-almond mixture. Spoon in remaining coffee mixture; sprinkle with remaining chocolate-almond mixture. Refrigerate 3 to 4 hours or until served. Makes 6 servings.

# Grapefruit & Kiwifruit Cups

| | |
|---|---|
| 3 large grapefruit, halved | 4 to 6 tablespoons brown sugar |
| 4 or 5 kiwifruit, peeled, thinly sliced | |
| 6 to 8 tablespoons medium sherry or Madeira | |

1. Using a grapefruit knife, remove grapefruit sections. Set aside. Remove and discard membranes. Reserve shells.
2. Line grapefruit shells with kiwifruit slices. Spoon grapefruit sections into center; sprinkle with sherry or Madeira and sugar to taste.
3. Refrigerate 1 hour. Makes 6 servings.

Left to right: Grapefruit & Kiwifruit Cups, Soufflé Olivia, Salmon en Croûte, Hollandaise Sauce, Almond Tuiles

*Partridges for Christmas*

Roast Partridges with Crunchy Stuffing Balls*
Green Soup*
Buttered Potatoes
Herbed Green Beans
Chocolate-Chestnut Gâteau*

*Recipe included in book

# Green Soup

| | |
|---|---|
| 1/4 cup butter or margarine | 1 teaspoon Worcester-shire sauce |
| 2 large leeks, sliced | Pinch of ground mace |
| 12 oz. Brussels sprouts, shredded | Salt |
| 5 cups chicken stock | Freshly ground pepper |
| 1 tablespoon lemon juice | 2 cups milk or half and half |

**1.** Melt butter or margarine in a large saucepan over medium heat. Add leeks; sauté 5 minutes, stirring occasionally.
**2.** Stir in Brussels sprouts. Stir in stock, lemon juice, Worcestershire sauce and mace. Season with salt and pepper. Bring to a boil.
**3.** Reduce heat. Cover pan; simmer 15 to 20 minutes or until vegetables are tender. Cool slightly. In a blender or food processor fitted with a steel blade, process mixture until pureed.
**4.** Pour pureed soup into a clean saucepan. Stir in milk or half and half. Heat until hot. Serve soup in warmed soup bowls. Makes 6 servings.

# Chocolate-Chestnut Gâteau

*Cake:*
1 (15-1/2-oz.) can chestnut puree
1 teaspoon vanilla extract
5 eggs, separated
1-3/4 cups sifted powdered sugar
2/3 cup sifted cake flour
1/4 cup unsweetened cocoa powder

*Filling:*
1 recipe Crème Pâtissière, page 56

3 tablespoons dark rum
1/2 pint whipping cream (1 cup)
2 tablespoons powdered sugar

*To decorate:*
4 oz. semisweet chocolate, shaved into curls
Marzipan Holly Leaves & Berries, page 14

**1.** Preheat oven to 350F (175C). Grease a deep 8-inch-round cake pan or springform pan. Line bottom and side of pan with waxed paper; grease paper.
**2.** To make cake, divide chestnut puree in half. Set 1/2 aside to use in filling. In a blender or food processor fitted with a steel blade, process remaining chestnut puree until smooth. Add vanilla, egg yolks and 1 cup powdered sugar; process until blended. Pour chestnut mixture into a large bowl.
**3.** Sift flour and cocoa over chestnut mixture; fold in.
**4.** In a medium bowl, beat egg whites until stiff but not dry. Gradually beat in remaining 3/4 cup powdered sugar; beat until stiff and glossy. Stir about 1/3 of beaten egg-white mixture into chestnut mixture. Fold in remaining egg-white mixture. Pour mixture into prepared pan; smooth top.
**5.** Bake in preheated oven 60 to 65 minutes or until a wooden pick inserted in center comes out clean. Cool in pan on a wire rack 10 minutes. Remove from pan; peel off lining paper. Cool completely on wire rack. Cut cooled cake horizontally into 3 layers.
**6.** To make filling, prepare Crème Pâtissière according to directions on page 56. Refrigerate until chilled.
**7.** Place 1 cake layer on a serving plate; spread with 1/2 of chilled Crème Pâtissière. Top with another cake layer; sprinkle with rum.
**8.** In a blender or food processor fitted with a steel blade, process reserved chestnut puree until smooth. Divide puree in half. Beat 1/2 of chestnut puree into remaining Crème Pâtissière until blended. Spread over second cake layer. Top with remaining cake layer.
**9.** In a medium bowl, beat cream until soft peaks form. Beat in powdered sugar. Spread whipped-cream mixture around side and over top of cake. Press chocolate around side of cake.
**10.** Spoon remaining chestnut puree into a pastry bag fitted with a medium star tip. Pipe in a lacy pattern on top of cake. Decorate cake with holly leaves and berries. Refrigerate 1 hour or until served. Makes 8 to 10 servings.

Right to left: Chocolate-Chestnut Gâteau, Green Soup, Roast Partridges with Crunchy Stuffing Balls

## Roast Partridges with Crunchy Stuffing Balls

6 lemon wedges
6 partridges, oven-ready
1/4 cup butter or
    margarine
Salt
Freshly ground pepper
12 bacon slices
2 tablespoons vegetable
    oil
1 cup red wine
6 bread slices, crusts
    removed
3 tablespoons orange
    marmalade
1 to 2 tablespoons lemon
    juice

*Stuffing Balls:*
2 tablespoons butter or
    margarine

1 onion, chopped
1-1/2 cups fresh bread
    crumbs
Grated peel of 1/2 lemon
1/3 cup chopped pecans
1 apple, peeled, cored,
    coarsely grated
Salt
Freshly ground pepper
2 tablespoons chopped
    fresh parsley
1/4 teaspoon dried leaf
    thyme
1 egg, beaten

*To garnish:*
Green grapes
Watercress sprigs

**1.** Preheat oven to 425F (220C). Place a lemon wedge inside each partridge. Rub each partridge all over with butter or margarine. Season with salt and pepper. Place partridges on a rack in a large roasting pan. Crisscross 2 slices of bacon over each partridge.
**2.** Roast in preheated oven 20 minutes, basting once. In a small saucepan, bring wine to a boil; pour over partridges. Roast 30 minutes more or until partridges are tender, basting once or twice with pan drippings.
**3.** Grease a baking sheet. To make stuffing balls, melt butter or margarine in a small saucepan over low heat. Add onion; sauté 7 minutes or until soft and lightly browned. Remove from heat. Stir in bread crumbs, lemon peel, pecans, apple, salt, pepper, parsley and thyme. Stir in egg until combined. Form mixture into 12 balls. Place on greased baking sheet; bake in oven with partridges 20 minutes or until browned.
**4.** Toast bread; place 1 toasted slice on each plate. Place a partridge on each toast slice; keep warm.
**5.** Remove and discard excess fat from roasting pan. Stir marmalade into pan juices; simmer about 5 minutes or until syrupy. Add lemon juice to taste.
**6.** Arrange hot stuffing balls around partridges. Garnish with small bunches of grapes and watercress sprigs. Serve sauce separately. Makes 6 servings.

**Special Dinner for 10**

Orange & Crab Cups*
Cornish Hens in
Red Wine with Chestnuts*
Scalloped Potatoes*
Tangy Red Cabbage*
Shortbread-Meringue Gâteau
Chocolate & Rum Mousse*

*Recipe included in book

# Orange & Crab Cups

2 (6-oz.) packages frozen
  crabmeat, thawed
2 (14-oz.) cans cut
  asparagus, drained
3/4 cup mayonnaise
1/4 cup whipping cream

1/4 cup dry sherry
2 tablespoons lemon juice
Salt
Freshly ground white
  pepper
5 medium oranges

1. In a medium bowl, break crabmeat into chunks. Stir in asparagus.
2. In a medium bowl, combine mayonnaise, whipping cream, sherry, lemon, salt and pepper. Gently stir into crab mixture.
3. Cut oranges in half; scoop out sections. Remove and discard membranes. Stir orange sections into crab mixture.
4. Place an orange shell on each individual plate. Spoon crab mixture into oranges. Refrigerate until served. Makes 10 servings.

# Cornish Hens in Red Wine with Chestnuts

5 Cornish hens, oven
  ready
Salt
Freshly ground pepper
3 tablespoons vegetable
  oil
2 large onions, sliced
2 tablespoons all-purpose
  flour
1-1/2 cups red wine
1-1/2 cups beef stock
1 tablespoon honey
3 tablespoons brandy,
  if desired
1 bay leaf
1 (15-oz.) can whole
  peeled chestnuts,
  drained

*Stuffing Balls:*
2 onions, finely chopped
2 celery stalks, finely
  chopped
1/4 cup butter or
  margarine
2 tablespoons chopped
  fresh parsley
2 teaspoons dried leaf
  thyme
5 cups fresh bread crumbs
2 eggs, beaten
Lemon juice, if desired

*To garnish:*
Parsley sprigs

1. Preheat oven to 350F (175C). Season hens with salt and pepper. Place in a large roasting pan.
2. Heat oil in a medium skillet over medium heat. Add onions; sauté about 7 minutes or until lightly browned. Stir in flour; cook 1 minute, stirring. Gradually stir in wine and stock; bring to a boil. Stir in honey and brandy, if desired. Season with salt and pepper. Add bay leaf. Simmer 2 minutes. Add chestnuts; spoon mixture over hens. Cover with foil.
3. Roast in preheated oven about 1-1/4 hours or until hens are tender.
4. Meanwhile make stuffing balls. Grease a large baking sheet. Melt butter or margarine in a medium skillet over low heat. Add onion and celery; sauté until soft. In a large bowl, combine onions, herbs and bread crumbs. Stir in eggs and lemon juice, if desired. Form mixture into 20 balls.
5. Arrange stuffing balls close together on greased baking sheet. Bake with hens 30 minutes or until browned.
6. Place hens on a large warmed serving dish; keep warm. Discard bay leaf from pan. With a slotted spoon, remove chestnuts from cooking juices. Arrange chestnuts and stuffing balls around hens. Garnish with parsley sprigs. Serve pan juices separately. Makes 10 servings.

**Variation**
Bake stuffing balls after removing hens from oven. Cover hens with foil to keep warm.

# Scalloped Potatoes

**4 lb. potatoes, peeled,
    thinly sliced**
**3 onions, thinly sliced**
**Salt**
**Freshly ground pepper**

**2 cups beef stock**
**2 tablespoons butter or
    margarine, melted**
**2 tablespoons chopped
    fresh parsley**

**1.** Preheat oven to 350F (175C). Generously grease a 2-quart baking dish. Layer potatoes and onions in greased dish, ending with potatoes; season with salt and pepper.
**2.** In a small saucepan over medium heat, bring stock to boil. Pour boiling stock over potatoes and onions. Brush potatoes with butter or margarine. Cover with foil or a lid.
**3.** Bake in preheated oven 1-1/2 hours. Remove foil; bake 30 minutes or until potatoes are tender and lightly browned.
**4.** If desired, for a browner top, place under a broiler until potatoes are well browned and crispy on top. Sprinkle with parsley. Serve hot. Makes 10 servings.

Left to right: Cornish Hens in Red Wine with Chestnuts; Tangy Red Cabbage, page 56; Scalloped Potatoes

# Tangy Red Cabbage

| | |
|---|---|
| 2 tablespoons vegetable oil | 1/4 cup red-wine vinegar |
| 1 large onion, thinly sliced | 1/4 cup water |
| 12 cups finely shredded red cabbage (about 3 lb.) | 3 tablespoons light-brown sugar |
| 1 large apple, peeled, cored, chopped | Salt |
| | Freshly ground pepper |

**1.** Heat oil in a large saucepan over medium heat. Add onion; sauté about 5 minutes or until softened.
**2.** Add cabbage, apple, vinegar and water to pan. Stir to combine. Cook, stirring frequently, until cabbage begins to soften. Stir in sugar; season with salt and pepper. Cover and simmer 30 to 40 minutes or until cabbage is tender, stirring occasionally. Add more water, if necessary to prevent sticking.
**3.** Spoon into a serving dish. Makes 10 servings.

# Shortbread-Meringue Gâteau

**Meringue:**
2 egg whites
1/4 cup granulated sugar
1/3 cup firmly packed light-brown sugar

**Shortbread:**
1/2 cup butter or margarine room temperature
1/2 cup firmly packed light-brown sugar
2 cups all-purpose flour
1/4 cup cornstarch

**Crème Pâtissière:**
1/3 cup sugar
2 tablespoons all-purpose flour

2 tablespoons cornstarch
1-1/4 cups milk
2 egg yolks
1 teaspoon vanilla extract
1 tablespoon butter or margarine

**Topping:**
1 (29-oz.) can apricot halves, drained
1/2 pint whipping cream (1 cup)
2 tablespoons powdered sugar

**To decorate:**
Angelica

**1.** Preheat oven to 225F (105C). Line a baking sheet with parchment paper. Draw a 9-inch circle on parchment paper.

**2.** To make meringue, in a medium bowl, beat egg whites until stiff peaks form. Beat in sugars, 1 tablespoon at a time, beating constantly until meringue is stiff and glossy. Spoon meringue into a pastry bag fitted with a large star tip. Pipe inside circle on parchment paper, filling completely.
**3.** Bake in preheated oven 2 hours or until crisp and dry. Cool on baking sheet on a wire rack 10 minutes. Peel off paper; cool completely on wire rack.
**4.** Increase oven temperature to 350F (175C). To make shortbread, line a baking sheet with parchment paper. Grease bottom of a 9-1/2-inch fluted quiche pan or tart pan with a removable bottom. In a medium bowl, beat butter or margarine and brown sugar until light and fluffy. Sift flour and cornstarch over sugar mixture; stir in.
**5.** Divide dough into 2 pieces, making 1 piece 2/3 of dough. On a lightly floured surface, roll out small piece of dough to 3/8 inch thick. Cut out 10 (2-inch) circles with a floured 2-inch fluted cookie cutter. Place circles on lined baking sheet; prick tops with a fork.
**6.** Pat out large piece of dough on bottom of prepared pan, pressing dough into fluted edges of pan. Smooth top; prick with a fork.
**7.** Bake cookies in preheated oven 15 to 18 minutes. Bake shortbread base 30 to 35 minutes or until golden brown. Cool cookies on baking sheet on a wire rack 10 minutes. Remove from paper; cool completely on wire rack. Cool shortbread base completely in pan on wire rack. Remove cooled shortbread from pan, sliding off bottom of pan.
**8.** To make Crème Pâtissière, in a medium saucepan, combine sugar, flour and cornstarch. Stir in milk until blended. Cook over medium heat, stirring constantly, until mixture thickens and comes to a boil. Remove from heat. Beat egg yolks in a small bowl. Add 1/4 cup hot milk mixture to beaten egg yolks; stir until blended. Return mixture to saucepan; stir well. Cook, stirring constantly, until mixture thickens. Do not boil. Remove from heat; stir in vanilla and butter or margarine.
**9.** Pour into a medium bowl; place a sheet of waxed paper on surface of custard to prevent a skin from forming. Refrigerate 2 to 3 hours or until chilled.
**10.** To make topping, reserve 10 apricot halves for decoration. Coarsely chop remaining apricot halves. Drain on paper towels; set aside. In a medium bowl, beat cream until soft peaks form. Beat in powdered sugar. Fold 1/2 of whipped-cream mixture and reserved chopped apricots into chilled custard. Spoon remaining whipped-cream mixture into a pastry bag fitted with a large star tip.
**11.** To serve, place shortbread base on a serving plate; cover with apricot-cream mixture. Place meringue on top. Pipe whipped-cream mixture alternately in 10 large swirls and 10 small swirls around edge of meringue. Decorate small swirls with reserved apricot halves and large swirls with shortbread cookies. Decorate center with angelica strips. Refrigerate up to 4 hours or until served. Makes 8 to 10 servings.

# Chocolate & Rum Mousse

**12 oz. semisweet chocolate, chopped**
**3 tablespoons water**
**2 to 3 tablespoons dark rum**
**3/4 cup butter or margarine, cut into pieces**
**6 eggs, separated**

**3/4 cup granulated sugar**
**3/4 cup whipping cream**
**1 tablespoon powdered sugar**

*To decorate:*
**Stem ginger, if desired**

1. Melt chocolate in a small heavy saucepan over very low heat; stir until smooth. Stir in water and rum to taste until blended. Stir in butter or margarine, a few pieces at a time, until melted. Let cool.

2. In a medium bowl, beat egg yolks and granulated sugar until thick and lemon-colored. Add chocolate mixture in a slow steady stream, beating until thoroughly blended. Refrigerate until completely cool.

3. In a medium bowl, beat egg whites until stiff but not dry. Stir 1/3 of beaten egg whites into cooled chocolate mixture. Fold in remaining beaten egg whites until no streaks remain.

4. Pour mixture into 10 serving dishes or wine glasses; refrigerate several hours or until firm.

5. To serve, beat cream in a medium bowl until soft peaks form. Beat in powdered sugar. Decorate each serving with swirls of whipped cream; add pieces of stem ginger, if desired. Serve with small cookies, if desired. Makes 10 servings.

Clockwise from left: Chocolate & Rum Mousse;
Shortbread-Meringue Gâteau; Almond Macaroons, page 20

*Low-Calorie Christmas*

Sunchoke Soup*
Turkey & Spinach
Rolls*
Steamed Rice
Green Beans
Red-Fruit Salad with
Fluffy Yogurt*

*Recipe included in book

## Sunchoke Soup

| | |
|---|---|
| 1 large onion, chopped | Salt |
| 2 lb. sunchokes (Jerusalem artichokes), peeled, sliced | Freshly ground pepper |
| | 1 to 2 tablespoons lemon juice |
| 4-1/2 cups chicken stock | 1/2 cup milk |
| 1 bay leaf | Chopped fresh parsley |
| Pinch of mace | |

1. In a large saucepan, combine onion, sunchokes, stock, bay leaf and mace. Season with salt and pepper. Bring to a boil; reduce heat. Cover and simmer about 30 minutes or until tender.
2. Discard bay leaf. In a blender or food processor fitted with a steel blade, process soup until smooth.
3. Pour puree into a clean saucepan; add lemon juice to taste. Bring to a boil; stir in milk. Reduce heat; simmer 2 to 3 minutes. Serve soup in warmed soup bowls. Sprinkle with parsley. Has about 50 calories per serving. Makes 6 servings.

## Turkey & Spinach Rolls

| | |
|---|---|
| 6 (4- to 5-oz.) turkey fillets | Grated peel of 1/2 lemon, if desired |
| Salt | 2 teaspoons cornstarch |
| Freshly ground pepper | 1/2 cup plain yogurt |
| Ground coriander | 1 teaspon brown mustard |
| 18 to 24 fresh spinach leaves, stalks removed | 1 egg yolk |
| 1 onion, very finely sliced | |
| 1-1/2 cups chicken stock | *To garnish:* |
| 1-1/2 cups thinly sliced mushrooms (about 8 oz.) | Parsley sprigs |
| | Carrot sticks |
| | Celery sticks |

1. Preheat oven to 350F (175C). Grease a shallow casserole large enough to hold turkey rolls in 1 layer. Slice fillets almost in half horizontally; open out. Lay flat between 2 sheets of plastic wrap; pound until 1/8 inch thick. Season with salt, pepper and coriander.
2. Evenly arrange spinach leaves over pounded fillets. Place onion slices on spinach; roll up fillets. Fasten with wooden picks.
3. Arrange turkey rolls, seam-side down, close together, in greased casserole.
4. In a medium saucepan, bring stock to a boil. Season with salt and pepper. Pour hot stock over turkey rolls. Add remaining onion slices. Cover with a lid or foil.
5. Bake in preheated oven 45 to 60 minutes or until turkey is tender. Remove turkey rolls with a slotted spoon. Remove and discard wooden picks. Place turkey rolls on a serving dish; keep warm.
6. Strain cooking liquid into a medium saucepan; boil until reduced to about 1 cup. Add mushrooms and lemon peel, if desired.
7. In a small bowl, blend cornstarch, yogurt, mustard and egg yolk. Stir in a little of hot mixture. Return to saucepan; stir well. Simmer 2 to 3 minutes, stirring constantly. Spoon sauce over turkey rolls.
8. Garnish turkey rolls with parsley sprigs and carrot and celery sticks. Serve with green beans and steamed rice, if desired. Each turkey roll has about 210 calories per serving. Makes 6 servings.

## Fluffy Yogurt

| | |
|---|---|
| 3/4 cup plain yogurt | 1 egg white |
| 1 teaspoon vanilla extract | |

1. Spoon yogurt into a small bowl; stir until smooth. Stir in vanilla.
2. In a small bowl, beat egg white until stiff but not dry; fold beaten egg white into yogurt. Serve as a topping for Red-Fruit Salad, opposite. Has about 5 calories per tablespoon. Makes 1-1/2 cups.

# Red-Fruit Salad

**1 (15-oz.) can black
  cherries, pitted**
**1/2 cup apple juice**
**4 medium pears, peeled,
  cored, sliced**
**8 oz. frozen raspberries**

**6 oz. black grapes,
  halved, seeded**

*To serve:*
**Fluffy Yogurt, opposite**

**1.** Drain syrup from cherries into a medium saucepan. Place cherries into a serving bowl. Add apple juice to cherry juice.
**2.** Add pears to saucepan. Bring to a boil. Reduce heat; simmer about 3 to 4 minutes or until pears are almost tender. Remove from heat. Add raspberries to pears; stir until thawed. Spoon mixture into cherries.
**4.** Stir in grapes; refrigerate until chilled. Serve with Fluffy Yogurt. Has about 140 calories per serving without yogurt. Makes 6 servings.

Clockwise from top: Red-Fruit Salad, Green beans, Turkey & Spinach Rolls

# Alternative Main Dishes

## Whiskey Steaks Dijon

6 beef-loin tenderloin
   steaks (4 to 6 oz. each)
Salt
Freshly ground pepper
1 garlic clove, crushed
1/4 cup butter or
   margarine
2 tablespoons vegetable
   oil
1-1/2 cups sliced
   mushrooms (about
   8 oz.)

5 tablespoons whiskey
2 tablespoons Dijon-style
   mustard
1 cup beef stock

*To garnish:*
Watercress sprigs

1. Season steaks with salt, pepper and garlic.
2. Heat butter or margarine in a large skillet over medium-high heat. Add steaks; sauté 2 to 3 minutes on each side. Cook 1 to 3 minutes more on each side or to desired doneness. Remove from skillet; keep warm.
3. Add mushrooms to drippings in skillet; sauté 1 to 2 minutes. Stir in whiskey, mustard and stock. Bring to a boil, stirring constantly. Season with salt and pepper. Return steaks to skillet; turn to coat with sauce. Place on a warmed serving dish; spoon sauce over steak. Garnish with watercress sprigs.
4. Serve hot with sautéed potatoes or baked potatoes and buttered carrots, green beans or broccoli. Makes 6 servings.

## Traditional Roast Beef

1 (4- to 5-lb.) beef rib
   roast
Salt
Freshly ground pepper

*Yorkshire Pudding:*
3/4 cup all-purpose flour
1/2 teaspoon salt
1 cup milk
2 eggs

1. Preheat oven to 325F (165C). Place roast on a rack in a roasting pan. Season with salt and pepper.
2. Roast in preheated oven about 2 hours for medium doneness or to desired doneness. Transfer roast to a warmed serving dish. Reserve 1/4 cup drippings.
3. Add reserved drippings to a 13" x 9" pan or a muffin pan. Heat until hot.
4. To make Yorkshire pudding, increase oven temperature to 400F (205C). Sift flour and salt into a medium bowl. Beat in eggs and milk to make a smooth batter. Pour batter into hot drippings.
5. Bake in preheated oven about 20 minutes. Reduce heat to 350F (175C); bake 10 to 15 minutes or until puffed and golden brown.
6. Serve roast with Yorkshire pudding. Serve with Brussels sprouts tossed with toasted almonds or cauliflower with cheese sauce. Degrease and serve pan juices separately. Reheat if necessary. Makes about 8 servings.

Left to right: Brussels sprouts with almonds, Traditional Roast Beef with Yorkshire Puddings

# Baked Ham with Ginger Glaze

1 (4-lb.) smoked cook-
    before-eating ham
1-1/2 cups ginger ale
3 tablespoons orange
    marmalade

6 tablespoons dark-
    brown sugar

**1.** Preheat oven to 325F (165C). Place ham in a roasting pan. Add ginger ale. Cover roasting pan tightly with foil.
**2.** Bake in preheated oven 1-1/2 hours, basting occasionally.
**3.** Remove ham from oven. Increase oven temperature to 400F (205C). Carefully remove any skin from ham. Score fat in a diamond pattern. In a small bowl, combine marmalade and sugar; spread over scored fat.
**4.** Bake 30 minutes more. Ham should reach an internal temperature of 160F (70C).
**5.** Serve hot or cold. Thicken pan juices with a little corn-starch mixed with cold water, if desired. Makes 6 to 8 servings.

Duck with Orange & Brandy Sauce, Bacon-topped cauliflower

# Duck with Orange & Brandy Sauce

| | |
|---|---|
| 2 (5- to 6-lb.) ducks, oven-ready | 1 tablespoon all-purpose flour |
| 1 onion, coarsely chopped | 1/2 cup white wine |
| Salt | 3 tablespoons brandy |
| Freshly ground pepper | 2 tablespoons red-currant jelly |
| 3 tablespoons butter or margarine | 1 to 2 tablespoons honey |
| 2 tablespoons vegetable oil | *To garnish:* |
| 3 oranges | Orange slices |
| 1 lemon | Parsley sprigs |
| About 1/2 cup beef stock | Green onions |

1. Preheat oven to 375F (190C). Remove and discard excess fat and giblets. Prick skin all over with a fork to allow fat to escape during roasting. Sprinkle with salt and pepper. Place ducks, breast-side up, in a shallow roasting pan.
2. Roast ducks in preheated oven about 1-1/2 hours, basting frequently, until tender or to 180F (85C) on a meat thermometer. Juices should run clear when duck is pierced between thigh and breast.
3. Meanwhile, peel 2 oranges; cut peel into thin strips. In a medium saucepan; cook peel, in water to cover, 8 to 10 minutes or until tender. Drain peel; reserve 1/2 cup of cooking liquid.
4. Squeeze juice from all oranges and lemon into a measuring cup. Add enough stock to make 1 cup.
5. Place ducks on a warmed serving plate; keep warm. Skim off and discard fat from roasting pan. Whisk flour into roasting pan; cook 1 to 2 minutes, stirring.
6. Gradually stir in reserved orange-peel cooking liquid, stock mixture, wine and brandy; bring to a boil. Stir in jelly and honey. Season with salt and pepper. Cook until jelly melts, stirring. Boil until reduced by about 1/4.
7. Sprinkle 1/2 of orange strips over ducks. Pour sauce into a warmed sauce dish; stir in remaining orange strips. Serve sauce separately.
8. Garnish ducks with orange slices, parsley sprigs and green onions. Makes about 8 servings.

# Leg of Lamb

| | |
|---|---|
| 1 (5- to 6-lb.) lamb leg roast, boneless | 2 cups beef stock |
| 1 garlic clove, cut in half | 2 tablespoons red-currant jelly |
| Salt | 3 tablespoons medium sherry |
| Freshly ground pepper | 1 tablespoon tomato paste |
| Fresh rosemary sprigs | |
| *Gravy:* | |
| 1/4 cup all-purpose flour | |

1. Preheat oven to 325F (165C).
2. Rub lamb all over with cut side of garlic; discard garlic. Season with salt and pepper. Place lamb in a large roasting pan. Add rosemary to pan.
3. Roast in preheated oven about 3 hours for medium done, 160F (70C) on a meat thermometer, or to desired doneness.
4. Place lamb on a serving plate; keep warm. Discard rosemary.
5. To make gravy, spoon off all fat except about 3 tablespoons from pan. Stir in flour. Cook 2 to 3 minutes, stirring, until lightly browned. Gradually stir in stock, jelly, sherry and tomato paste. Bring to a boil; season with salt and pepper. Simmer 2 minutes. Strain into a warmed sauce dish. Serve sauce separately. Makes 6 to 8 servings.

# Venison en Croûte

1 (4- to 5-lb.) rolled
  venison rump roast
6 bacon slices
Salt
Freshly ground pepper

*Sauce:*
3 tablespoons all-purpose
  flour
1-1/2 cups beef stock
4 or 5 tablespoons port
3 tablespoons red-currant
  jelly
2 to 3 teaspoons
  lemon juice

*Stuffing:*
3 tablespoons butter or
  margarine

1 onion, chopped
1-1/2 cups chopped
  mushrooms (about
  8 oz.)
3/4 cup fresh bread
  crumbs
1 teaspoon prepared
  brown mustard
3/4 teaspoon dried
  leaf basil
1 (17-1/2-oz.) pkg. frozen
  puff pastry, thawed
1 egg, beaten

*To garnish:*
Watercress sprigs

1. Preheat oven to 400F (205C). Arrange bacon slices over and around roast; tie in place with kitchen string. Place venison on a rack in a roasting pan. Season with salt and pepper.
2. Roast venison in preheated oven 1-1/4 hours, basting several times. Place on a platter; cool slightly. Refrigerate until completely cool.
3. To make sauce, skim any excess fat from pan drippings. Whisk flour into juices; cook, stirring, 1 to 2 minutes. Gradually stir in stock; bring to a boil. Stir in port, jelly, lemon juice and salt and pepper to taste. Cook until jelly dissolves. Strain sauce into a saucepan; cover and refrigerate.
4. To make stuffing, melt butter or margarine in a medium saucepan over low heat. Add onion; sauté until soft and lightly browned. Stir in mushrooms; cook 1 to 2 minutes. Remove from heat; stir in bread crumbs, mustard and basil. Cool slightly.

5. Preheat oven to 400F (205C). When roast is cold, remove bacon and string. On a lightly floured surface, roll out pastry large enough to enclose roast, joining 2 pieces into 1. Reserve trimming for decorations, if desired. Spread stuffing down center of pastry; place roast in center. Wrap roast in pastry, sealing edges with water. Place, seam-side down, in a lightly greased baking pan; brush with egg to glaze. Cut leaves from pastry trimmings, if desired. Place pastry leaves on pastry; brush with egg.
6. Bake in preheated oven 30 minutes. Reduce oven temperature to 350F (175C). Bake 1 hour more. Cover pastry with foil if it browns too rapidly.
7. Reheat sauce; pour into a warmed sauce dish. Place venison on a serving dish; garnish with watercress sprigs. Serve with creamed potatoes or Duchess Potatoes, page 48; and spinach and buttered carrots. Makes 8 servings.

**Variation**
**Beef en Croûte:** Substitute a boneless beef round rump roast for vension.

Venison en Croûte with Duchess Potatoes, page 48

# Stuffed Pork Roast

1 (5- to 6-lb.) boneless
    pork shoulder-blade roast
Salt
Freshly ground pepper

*Stuffing:*
1 (10-oz.) pkg. frozen
    chopped spinach, thawed
2 tablespoons butter or
    margarine
1 onion, finely chopped

1 cup diced cooked ham
1 cup fresh bread crumbs
1/2 cup coarsely chopped
    walnuts
Salt
Freshly ground pepper
1 egg, beaten

*To serve:*
Applesauce
Steamed broccoli

**1.** Preheat oven to 325F (165C). Unroll roast; season with salt and pepper.
**2.** Drain thawed spinach thoroughly; place in a large bowl.
**3.** Melt butter or margarine in a medium skillet over low heat. Add onion and ham; sauté, stirring frequently, about 5 minutes or until lightly browned. Add ham mixture, bread crumbs and walnuts to spinach. Season with salt and pepper; stir in egg.
**4.** Spread stuffing over unrolled roast. Reroll; tie securely with kitchen string. Place roast on a rack in a roasting pan.
**5.** Roast in preheated oven about 3-1/2 hours or to an internal temperature of 170F (75C).
**6.** Serve roast with applesauce and broccoli. Makes 8 to 10 servings.

## Christmas-Tree Cake

1 (8-inch) square
fruitcake or Lemon
Cake, page 72,
covered with marzipan
and iced with 2 coats of
Royal Icing
1 yard red or green
ribbon, 1-inch wide
1/3 recipe Royal Icing,
using 1 egg white,
page 70

9 marzipan Christmas
Trees with red tubs,
page 14
Silver dragrees
3 Marzipan Holly Leaves
& Berries, page 14,
if desired

1. Make sure that cake icing is dry before you start to decorate it and that it is firmly attached with icing to a cake board about 2 inches larger than cake.
2. Carefully arrange ribbon over cake as in photo; attach with pins or dabs of icing.
3. Half-fill a pastry bag fitted with a small writing tip with icing. Between ribbon and edge of cake, pipe a straight line parallel to and about 1/4 inch from ribbon; see photo. Pipe additional lines at about 1/2-inch intervals to edge of cake. Repeat on other side.
4. Turn cake; starting at cake edge, pipe across first lines parallel to edge of cake. Pipe lines from edge of ribbon to edge of cake; see photo. Pipe 2 lines close together. Leave about a 1/2-inch space between sets of lines. Repeat to form 2 lattice triangles on each side of ribbons; see photo.
5. Trace the word 'NOEL' on top of cake between ribbons. Pipe a double row of icing over letters. Let dry. Pipe over letters; let dry.
6. Spoon remaining icing into a pastry bag fitted with a large writing tip; pipe a row of dots along inside edges of ribbons and along edges of cake. Let dry.
7. In center of each side, pipe 3 dots, graduated in size, down side of cake with 2 dots on each side. Except for front side, pipe a series of these dots at each end of cake sides; see photo.
8. Pipe a twisted continuous line all around bottom edge of cake. Pipe additional dots above edging to match those below top edge of cake. Let dry.
9. Attach silver dragrees to Christmas trees with a dab of icing. Let dry. With a dab of icing, attach Christmas trees to cake, 2 on each side and 1 on top of cake; see photo. Attach holly leaves and berries, if desired. Makes 8 to 10 servings.

## Lattice Christmas Cake

1 (8-inch) round
fruitcake or Lemon
Cake, page 66, covered
with marzipan and iced
with 2 coats of
Royal Icing
1/3 recipe Royal Icing,
using 1 egg white,
page 70
Red food coloring
About 1 yard red ribbon,
1-1/4 to 1-1/2 inches
wide

About 1 yard green
ribbon, 1/2 inch wide
8 to 12 Marzipan Holly
Leaves & Berries,
page 14
6 to 8 Marzipan Green
Leaves, page 14
5 to 7 molded Marzipan
Roses, page 15

1. Make sure that cake icing is dry before you start to decorate it and that it is firmly attached with icing to a cake board about 2 inches larger than cake.
2. Cut a 4-inch square of paper. Place on center of cake. Attach a number 2 plain writing tip to a pastry bag. Spoon icing into bag until half full. Pipe icing on 2 opposite sides of square, close to paper square, but not touching. Using a straight edge as a guide, extend ends of lines to edge of cake. Continue piping lines parallel to those already piped, making 5 to 7 parallel lines between square and edge of cake, keeping lines an equidistance apart. Do not pipe lines inside square. Let dry.
3. Turn cake a quarter turn; add lines as before but at right angles to those already piped. Let dry.
4. Tint a small amount of icing red. Spoon into a pastry bag fitted with a number 2 writing tip. On 2 sides of square, pipe over white lines across cake, making lines 2 layers deep. Then pipe over every other white line, as shown. Let dry.
5. Turn cake a quarter turn; repeat at right angles to complete lattice. Let dry.
6. Spoon white icing into a pastry bag fitted with a star tip. Pipe a twisted loop around top edge of cake. Pipe 2 stars under every other loop on side of cake.
7. Around bottom edge of cake, pipe large stars directly under small stars; pipe a small star above every other large star; see photo. Let dry.
8. Tie red and green ribbons around side of cake, finishing with a bow, if desired.
9. Decorate top of cake with 2 or 3 holly leaves and berries at each corner of square. Arrange roses, mistletoe leaves and berries in center, attaching with a dab of icing. Makes 8 to 10 servings.

**Variation**
To decorate a square cake with this design, position square in center of cake at right angles to shape of cake.

Top to bottom: Lattice Christmas Cake, Christmas-Tree Cake

# Light Fruitcake

1 cup currants
1 cup golden raisins
1/2 cup chopped mixed candied fruit
1/3 cup red candied cherries, chopped
1/3 cup ground almonds
1 cup butter or margarine, room temperature
1-1/4 cups sugar
4 eggs
1 tablespoon grated orange peel

1-3/4 cups all-purpose flour
1 teaspoon baking powder
1 teaspoon ground cinnamon
1/2 teaspoon grated nutmeg
1/2 teaspoon ground cloves
1/3 cup orange juice

1. Preheat oven to 300F (150C). Grease a deep 8-inch-round cake pan or springform pan. Line bottom and side of pan with waxed paper; grease paper.
2. In a medium bowl, combine currants, raisins, candied fruit, cherries and ground almonds; set aside.
3. In a large bowl, beat butter or margarine and sugar until light and fluffy. Beat in eggs, 1 at a time, beating well after each addition. Beat in orange peel.
4. Sift flour, baking powder, cinnamon, nutmeg and cloves into a medium bowl. Add to egg mixture alternately with orange juice; beat until blended. Fold in fruit mixture. Spoon into prepared pan; smooth top.
5. Bake in preheated oven 2 hours 15 minutes or until a wooden pick inserted in center comes out clean. Cool completely in pan on a wire rack. Remove from pan; peel off lining paper. Wrap cake in plastic wrap and foil. Store in a cool place until served. Makes 12 to 16 servings.

Left to right: Coffee & Walnut Cake, Almond Cake

# Coffee & Walnut Cake

**Cake:**
3/4 cup butter or margarine, room temperature
1 cup firmly packed light-brown sugar
3 eggs
1/4 cup strong black coffee
1/2 cup milk
1-3/4 cups self-rising flour, sifted
1/2 cup finely chopped walnuts

**Filling:**
1/4 cup butter or margarine, room temperature
1 cup powdered sugar, sifted
1 to 2 tablespoons strong black coffee

**Frosting:**
1-1/2 cups sugar
2 egg whites
1/2 teaspoon cream of tartar
1/8 teaspoon salt
3 tablespoons water
1 tablespoon strong black coffee

**To decorate:**
Walnut halves

1. Preheat oven to 350F (175C). Grease and flour 2 (8-inch) round cake pans.
2. To make cake, in a medium bowl, beat butter or margarine and brown sugar until light and fluffy. Beat in eggs, 1 at a time, beating well after each addition.
3. In a small bowl, combine coffee and milk. Add flour to egg mixture alternately with coffee mixture; beat until blended. Stir in walnuts. Pour batter into prepared pans; smooth tops.
4. Bake in preheated oven 35 to 40 minutes or until a wooden pick inserted in center comes out clean. Cool in pans on wire racks 5 minutes. Remove from pans; cool completely on wire racks.
5. To make filling, in a medium bowl, beat butter or margarine, powdered sugar and coffee until blended and smooth.
6. To make frosting, place sugar, egg whites, cream of tartar, salt, water and coffee in top of a double boiler; beat with an electric hand mixer 1 minute or until foamy. Place over a pan of simmering water; beat until mixture stands in soft peaks. Remove from heat; beat until frosting is fluffy.
7. Place 1 cooled cake layer, bottom-side up, on a serving plate; spread with filling. Top with second layer, top-side up. Spread frosting around side and over top of cake, swirling frosting. Decorate with walnut halves; let stand until frosting is set. Makes 6 to 8 servings.

# Almond Cake

**Cake:**
3/4 cup butter or margarine, room temperature
1 cup sugar
4 eggs
1 teaspoon almond extract
1-1/4 cups self-rising flour, sifted
3/4 cup finely ground blanched almonds

**Icing:**
2 oz. semisweet chocolate, chopped
3 tablespoons butter or margarine
1 egg yolk
1 cup powdered sugar, sifted

**To decorate:**
Whole blanched almonds, toasted

1. Preheat oven to 350F (175C). Grease a deep 8-inch-round cake pan. Line bottom and side of pan with waxed paper; grease paper.
2. To make cake, in a medium bowl, beat butter or margarine and sugar until light and fluffy. Beat in eggs, 1 at a time, beating well after each addition. Beat in almond extract.
3. Fold in flour and ground almonds. Spread mixture evenly in prepared pan.
4. Bake in preheated oven 60 to 70 minutes or until a wooden pick inserted in center comes out clean. Cool in pan on a wire rack 10 minutes. Remove from pan; remove lining paper. Cool completely on wire rack.
5. To make icing, melt chocolate and butter or margarine in a small heavy saucepan over low heat; stir until smooth. Let cool slightly. Beat in egg yolk; then beat in powdered sugar. Beat until icing is a good consistency for spreading.
6. Spread icing over top of cake; decorate with whole almonds. Makes 6 to 8 servings.

# Marzipan

1 lb. almond paste
1 teaspoon almond
  extract
3 tablespoons light corn
  syrup

4 cups sifted powdered
  sugar

### Mixer Method:

1. Break up almond paste; place in bowl of a heavy-duty mixer. Add almond extract and corn syrup. Beat on low speed until thoroughly blended.
2. Add powdered sugar gradually; beat until sugar is completely incorporated. Knead on a marble slab or other cold surface until smooth and pliable. Wrap in plastic wrap; refrigerate until needed. Allow marzipan to stand at room temperature before using.

### Food-Processor Method:

1. Break up almond paste. Process in a food processor fitted with a steel blade a few seconds. Add almond extract and corn syrup; process until blended.
2. Add powdered sugar, 1 cup at a time; process until sugar is incorporated, scraping down side of bowl as necessary. Knead on a marble slab or other cold surface until smooth and pliable. Wrap and store as directed above. Makes about 2 pounds marzipan or enough to cover an 8- or 9-inch-round or 9-inch-square fruitcake.

### How to Cover a Cake with Marzipan

1. Divide marzipan in half. On a surface lightly coated with powdered sugar, roll out 1/2 of marzipan until a little larger than top of cake. Or roll out 1/2 of marzipan between 2 sheets of plastic wrap. Cut a circle or square about 1/2 inch larger than top of cake. Set aside.
2. Cut 2 lengths of string, one the distance around cake and the other the exact height of cake. Using strings as a guide, roll out and cut remaining marzipan into a strip the height and width needed to fit cake.
3. Place cake on a cake board. Brush side and top of cake with sieved apricot jam. Place marzipan strip around cake. Smooth ends together with a small spatula.
4. Place marzipan circle on top of cake. Smooth edges together with a spatula. If marzipan is too moist, rub lightly with sifted powdered sugar.
5. Store cake, uncovered, at least 24 hours or until dry. If marzipan is still damp when icing is added, oils will seep into icing, causing unattractive stains.

# Royal Icing

3 egg whites
6 cups powdered sugar
  (about 1-1/2 lb.), sifted
2 to 3 teaspoons lemon
  juice

1 to 1-1/2 teaspoons
  glycerin, if desired

1. In a medium bowl, beat egg whites until soft peaks form. Gradually beat in powdered sugar.
2. Beat in enough lemon juice and glycerin, if desired, to make a good consistency for spreading.
3. Cover bowl with a damp cloth or transfer to an airtight container. Let stand 1 to 2 hours to allow any air bubbles to come to surface. Makes enough icing to cover an 8-inch round cake.

### How to Use Royal Icing

1. Place a dab of icing on a cake board or flat plate, top with cake. Place on a turntable or an up-turned plate. Spoon a quantity of icing in center of cake; spread smoothly with a small spatula.
2. Draw a long straight knife or spatula carefully and evenly across cake. Keep spatula or knife at a 30° angle. Take care not to press heavily or unevenly.
3. Remove surplus icing by running spatula around top of cake, holding it at right angles.
4. If not completely smooth, cover with a little more icing; draw spatula or ruler across cake again. Repeat until smooth. Let dry.
5. For a round cake, spread a thin layer of icing around sides; smooth with spatula.
6. Holding a scraper or a spatula at a 45° angle to cake, slowly rotate cake with your free hand, at same time moving scraper or spatula slowly and evenly around side of cake. Remove scraper fairly quickly at an angle, so that seam is not noticeable.
7. Lift any excess icing from top edge of cake with a spatula, again rotating cake. Let dry.
8. For a square cake, the best way to make even corners is to ice 2 opposite sides first; let dry before icing other 2 sides. Spread some icing on 1 side. Draw scraper or spatula toward you, keeping cake still to give an even finish, making smooth corners and edges. Repeat with opposite side; let dry. Repeat process with 2 remaining sides; let dry.
9. Add a second layer of icing in same way to sides and top of cake, making sure each layer is dry before adding next frosting layer.

# Happy Christmas Cake

| | |
|---|---|
| 1 (8-inch) round fruitcake or Lemon Cake, page 72, covered with marzipan | Sifted powdered sugar, if desired |
| 1-1/4 recipes Royal Icing, using 4 egg whites, opposite | 14 to 16 Royal-Icing Christmas Roses, page 15 |
| About 1 teaspoon strained lemon juice | About 24 Marzipan Holly Leaves & Berries, page 14 |
| Yellow food coloring | About 10 Marzipan Ivy Leaves, page 14 |

**1.** Attach cake to a 10-inch round cake board with dabs of icing. Ice top of cake with Royal Icing, giving it 2 coats. Let dry.
**2.** Put 2 tablespoons icing in a pastry bag fitted with a number 2 writing tip. On a piece of stiff paper, draw 1 large and 1 small crescent shape; see photo. Cut out patterns. Position crescents on cake; pipe an outline around patterns, leaving just enough space to remove patterns when dry. Keep pastry bag in a plastic bag to prevent drying.
**3.** Put 3 tablespoons icing in a bowl; add enough lemon juice to give a flowing consistency. Spoon icing into crescent shapes, filling them completely. Use a wooden pick to ease icing into corners and burst any air bubbles. Let dry.
**4.** Mark out and write 'Happy Christmas' in space between crescents with pastry bag. Let dry.
**5.** Tint a tablespoon of icing yellow; spoon into a pastry bag fitted with a number 2 tip. Pipe over 'Happy Christmas' with yellow frosting.
**6.** With reserved white icing and writing tip, pipe small dots on outlines of crescent shapes.
**7.** Thicken remaining icing with sifted powdered sugar, if necessary, to make it stand in stiff peaks.
**8.** Spread thickened icing thickly around side of cake. Using a small spatula, make peaks in icing; see photo. Let dry.
**9.** Arrange Christmas roses, ivy leaves, holly leaves and berries on crescents; see photo. Attach decorations with a dab of icing; let dry. Makes 8 to 10 servings.

Happy Christmas Cake

# Lemon Cake

1 cup butter or
  margarine, room
  temperature
1-1/4 cups sugar
4 eggs
4 teaspoons grated lemon
  peel

4 teaspoons lemon juice
1-1/2 cups self-rising
  flour
3/4 cup all-purpose flour

1. Preheat oven to 325F (165C). Grease a deep 8-inch-round cake pan. Line bottom and side of pan with waxed paper; grease paper.
2. In a large bowl, beat butter or margarine and sugar until light and fluffy. Beat in eggs, 1 at a time, beating well after each addition. Beat in lemon peel and lemon juice.
3. Sift flours over egg mixture; fold in. Spread mixture evenly in prepared pan; smooth top.
4. Bake in preheated oven 65 to 70 minutes or until golden brown and a wooden pick inserted in center comes out clean. Cool in pan on a wire rack 10 minutes. Remove from pan; peel off lining paper. Cool completely on wire rack. Cake may be wrapped and frozen up to 3 months. Makes 8 to 10 servings.

# Glazed Fruitcake

*Cake:*
1/2 cup chopped candied
  pineapple
1 cup red candied
  cherries, chopped
2 tablespoons chopped
  crystallized ginger
2 tablespoons chopped
  citron
1/3 cup chopped
  blanched almonds
1/2 cup chopped mixed
  candied fruit
1-3/4 cups all-purpose
  flour
1/4 cup cornstarch
1 teaspoon baking
  powder
1/2 teaspoon grated
  nutmeg

1 cup butter or
  margarine, room
  temperature
1 cup sugar
3 eggs
1 tablespoon grated
  orange peel
2 teaspoons grated lemon
  peel
1/3 cup orange juice

*Topping:*
1/4 cup apricot jam
Whole blanched Brazil
  nuts
Red candied cherries
Whole blanched almonds
Pecan halves
Angelica strips

1. Preheat oven to 300F (150C). Grease a deep 8-inch-round cake pan or springform pan. Line bottom and side of pan with waxed paper; grease paper.
2. To make cake, in a medium bowl, combine pineapple, cherries, crystallized ginger, citron, almonds and mixed fruit. Sprinkle 1/2 cup flour over fruit mixture; toss to coat with flour. Sift remaining 1-1/4 cups flour, cornstarch, baking powder and nutmeg into a medium bowl; set aside.
3. In a large bowl, beat butter or margarine and sugar until light and fluffy. Beat in eggs, 1 at a time, beating well after each addition. Beat in orange peel and lemon peel.
4. Add flour mixture to egg mixture alternately with orange juice; beat until blended. Fold in fruit-nut mixture. Spoon into prepared pan; smooth top.
5. Bake in preheated oven 2 hours to 2 hours 15 minutes or until a wooden pick inserted in center comes out clean. Cool in pan on a wire rack 20 minutes. Remove from pan; peel off lining paper. Cool completely on wire rack.
6. To make topping, press apricot jam through a sieve into a small saucepan. Cook over low heat, stirring, until jam is melted. Cool slightly. Brush jam over top of cooled cake; decorate cake with Brazil nuts, cherries, almonds, pecans and angelica. Brush jam over nuts and fruit; let stand until set. Store cake in an airtight container in a cool place until served. Makes 12 to 16 servings.

# Chocolate Layer Cake

1/2 cup butter or margarine
3/4 cup firmly packed light-brown sugar
1/3 cup light corn syrup
1-1/2 cups all-purpose flour
2/3 cup unsweetened cocoa powder
1 teaspoon baking soda
1 egg
3/4 cup milk

*Chocolate Icing:*
3 tablespoons unsweetened cocoa powder

3 tablespoons hot water
1/2 cup butter or margarine, room temperature
2 cups powdered sugar, sifted
1 tablespoon light corn syrup
1 teaspoon vanilla extract

*To garnish:*
Chocolate curls, below

1. Preheat oven to 350F (175C). Grease 3 (8-inch) round cake pans. Line bottoms with parchment or waxed paper; grease paper.
2. In a small saucepan over low heat, stir butter or margarine, brown sugar and corn syrup until smooth. Cool slightly.
3. Sift flour, cocoa and baking soda into a medium bowl. Add brown-sugar mixture; beat until thoroughly blended. Beat in egg. Beat in milk until blended. Pour batter into prepared pans; smooth tops.
4. Bake in preheated oven 20 to 25 minutes or until centers spring back when lightly pressed. Cool in pans on wire racks 5 minutes. Remove from pans; peel off lining paper. Cool completely on wire racks.
5. To make icing, in a small bowl, dissolve cocoa in hot water; stir until smooth. In a medium bowl, beat butter or margarine until fluffy. Add powdered sugar to butter or margarine alternately with dissolved cocoa; beat until blended. Beat in corn syrup and vanilla; beat until icing is a good consistency for spreading. If necessary, refrigerate a few minutes to firm. Spoon about 1/4 of icing into a pastry bag fitted with a large star tip; set aside.
6. Place 1 layer, bottom-side up, on a serving plate; spread with 1/3 of remaining icing. Top with second layer; spread with 1/3 of icing. Top with third layer, top-side up. Spread remaining icing over top layer. Pipe reserved icing in swirls around edge of cake. Decorate center of cake with chocolate curls. Let stand until icing is set. Makes 8 to 10 servings.

---

### Chocolate Curls

Chocolate curls can be made quickly by shaving a block of chocolate with a vegetable peeler. Or melt chocolate; pour melted chocolate onto a marble slab or other cold flat surface. Let stand until chocolate is just firm. Form chocolate into curls by pushing a large spatula or a thin-bladed knife at a slight angle under chocolate.

Left to right: Glazed Fruitcake, Lemon Cake, Chocolate Layer Cake

# Stollen
GERMANY

| | |
|---|---|
| 1 cup raisins | 1 teaspoon salt |
| 1/2 cup currants | 3/4 cup milk, scalded |
| 1/2 cup red candied cherries, chopped | 2 (1/4-oz.) pkgs. active dry yeast (2 tablespoons) |
| 1/3 cup chopped mixed candied fruit | 1/4 cup warm water (110F, 45C) |
| 2 tablespoons chopped citron | 1/2 teaspoon almond extract |
| 1/3 cup slivered almonds | 2 eggs, beaten |
| 3 tablespoons light or dark rum | About 4-1/2 cups all-purpose flour |
| 1/2 cup butter or margarine | 2 tablespoons butter or margarine |
| 3/4 cup plus 1 teaspoon granulated sugar | Powdered sugar |

**1.** In a medium bowl, combine raisins, currants, cherries, mixed fruit, citron and almonds. Stir in rum; set aside.
**2.** Add 1/2 cup butter or margarine, 3/4 cup granulated sugar and salt to warm milk; stir until butter or margarine melts. Cool to room temperature.
**3.** In a medium bowl, dissolve yeast and remaining 1 teaspoon granulated sugar in warm water. Let stand 5 to 10 minutes or until foamy. Stir yeast mixture into cooled milk mixture.
**4.** Stir in almond extract and eggs. Stir in 2-1/2 cups flour with a wooden spoon until combined. Stir in fruit-nut mixture and 1-1/2 cups flour or enough remaining flour to make a soft dough.
**5.** On a lightly floured surface, knead in enough remaining flour to make a stiff dough. Knead 8 to 10 minutes or until dough is smooth and elastic.
**6.** Clean and grease bowl. Place dough in greased bowl, turning to coat all sides. Cover with a slightly damp towel. Let rise in a warm place, free from drafts, until doubled in bulk.
**7.** Grease 2 baking sheets. Melt remaining 2 tablespoons butter or margarine; cool slightly. Punch down dough; divide in half. On a lightly floured surface, roll out 1 piece of dough to a 12" x 8" oval. Brush dough lightly with cooled butter or margarine. From a long side, fold dough almost in half. Place on greased baking sheet. Brush with melted butter or margarine. Repeat with remaining piece of dough. Cover with a dry towel; let rise until doubled in bulk.
**8.** Preheat oven to 375F (190C).
**9.** Bake in preheated oven 25 to 30 minutes or until golden brown and stollen sounds hollow when tapped on bottom. Remove from baking sheets; cool completely on wire racks. Dust with powdered sugar before serving. Makes 2 stollen.

# Christmas-Tree Cookies
SCANDINAVIA

| *Cookies:* | 1/2 teaspoon ground ginger |
|---|---|
| 1/2 cup butter or margarine | 1/2 teaspoon ground cinnamon |
| 1/3 cup molasses | |
| 1/2 cup sugar | *Icing:* |
| 1 egg yolk, beaten | 1 egg white |
| 2 tablespoons ground almonds | 1/8 teaspoon cream of tartar |
| 1-1/2 cups all-purpose flour | 1 teaspoon water |
| 1/2 teaspoon baking soda | About 1-3/4 cups powdered sugar, sifted |
| 1/2 teaspoon ground cardamom | |

**1.** In a medium saucepan over low heat, stir butter or margarine, molasses and sugar; stir until smooth. Remove from heat; cool slightly. Stir in egg yolk and ground almonds.
**2.** Sift flour, baking soda, cardamom, ginger and cinnamon over molasses mixture; fold in. Stir to make a smooth dough. Shape dough into a flattened ball; wrap in plastic wrap. Refrigerate 30 minutes.
**3.** Preheat oven to 375F (190C). Grease 2 baking sheets.
**4.** On a lightly floured surface, roll out dough to 1/4 inch thick. Cut dough with floured 2- to 3-inch assorted Christmas cookie cutters. Place cookies about 1 inch apart on greased baking sheets.
**5.** Bake in preheated oven 10 to 12 minutes or until just firm to the touch. Remove from oven; immediately poke a hole in top of each cookie with a metal skewer. Cool on baking sheets on wire racks 1 minute. Remove from baking sheets; cool completely on wire racks.
**6.** To make icing, in a medium bowl, beat egg white, cream of tartar and water until foamy. Gradually beat in powdered sugar; beat until icing is very stiff. If the weather is humid, add additional sugar. Spoon icing into a pastry bag fitted with a star tip. Pipe icing over each cookie as desired; see photo for ideas. Let stand until icing is set.
**7.** Insert colored string or yarn through holes in cookies; knot string. Hang cookies on a Christmas tree. Makes 30 to 36 cookies.

Top to bottom: Christmas-Tree Cookies, Stollen

# Bûche de Noël
FRANCE

**Cake:**
4 eggs
2/3 cup granulated sugar
1 teaspoon vanilla extract
1/2 cup all-purpose flour
1/4 cup unsweetened
  cocoa powder
2 tablespoons butter or
  margarine, melted,
  cooled
Powdered sugar

**Filling:**
1/2 (15-1/2 oz.) can
  chestnut puree
1/2 cup whipping cream
3 to 4 tablespoons
  powdered sugar

**Chocolate Buttercream:**
1/3 cup granulated sugar
1/4 cup water
2 egg yolks
3/4 cup unsalted butter
  or margarine
2 oz. semisweet
  chocolate, melted,
  cooled
Powdered sugar

**To decorate:**
Marzipan Holly Leaves
  & Berries, page 14

1. Preheat oven to 375F (190C). Grease a 13" x 9" baking pan. Line bottom and sides of pan with waxed paper; grease paper.
2. To make cake, place eggs and granulated sugar in a large bowl set over a pan of simmering water. Beat with an electric hand mixer until thick and lemon-colored. Mixture should fall in ribbons when beaters are lifted. Remove bowl from heat; beat until mixture is cool. Beat in vanilla.
3. Gradually sift flour and cocoa over egg mixture; fold in. Fold in butter or margarine until no streaks remain. Spread mixture evenly in prepared pan; smooth top.
4. Bake in preheated oven 18 to 20 minutes or until center springs back when lightly pressed.
5. Sprinkle a clean towel with powdered sugar. Invert cake onto sugared towel; remove pan. Peel off lining paper; trim crusty edges of cake. Starting from 1 short end, roll up cake in towel, jelly-roll style. Cool completely on a wire rack.
6. To make filling, in a blender or food processor fitted with a steel blade, process chestnut puree until smooth. Spoon into a medium bowl. In a small bowl, beat cream until soft peaks form. Beat in powdered sugar. Fold whipped-cream mixture into chestnut puree until blended.
7. Unroll cake; spread chestnut-cream mixture over cake to within 1/4 inch of edges. Reroll cake, without towel; place, seam-side down, on a serving plate.
8. To make buttercream, in a small heavy saucepan over medium heat, combine granulated sugar and water. Stir until sugar dissolves. Bring to a boil, stirring. Boil, without stirring, until to thread stage 230F (110C) on a candy thermometer.
9. Meanwhile, in a medium bowl, beat egg yolks until thick and lemon-colored. Pour sugar syrup in a thin steady stream over egg yolks, beating constantly. Beat until cool. In a small bowl, beat butter until light and fluffy. Gradually beat butter into egg-yolk mixture; beat until fluffy. Beat

in chocolate. Refrigerate until firm and a good consistency for spreading.
10. Spread buttercream over cake, covering cake completely. Score buttercream with tines of a fork to resemble bark. Refrigerate until served. Immediately before serving, sift powdered sugar over top of cake; decorate with marzipan holly leaves and berries. Makes 8 to 10 servings.

# Roast Goose
FRANCE

1 (7- to 9-lb.) goose,
  oven-ready

**Stuffing:**
3 tablespoons butter or
  margarine
1 onion, finely chopped
1 tablespoon dried sage
2 tablespoons chopped
  fresh parsley
2-1/2 cups fresh bread
  crumbs
Salt
Freshly ground pepper
1 egg, beaten

**Gravy:**
2-1/2 tablespoons
  all-purpose flour
1 cup dry white wine
1 cup chicken stock or
  stock from giblets
Lemon juice, if desired

**To garnish:**
Pearl onions, cooked
Carrots sticks, cooked
Parsley sprigs

1. If using a frozen goose, thaw before cooking. Remove giblets; reserve liver. Use remaining giblets for stock, if desired. Remove and discard excess fat.
2. Preheat oven to 350F (175C). To make stuffing, melt butter or margarine in a medium skillet over medium heat. Add onion; sauté until soft. Add goose liver; sauté until no longer pink inside. Spoon mixture into a medium bowl; let cool slightly. Coarsely chop cooked liver. Stir in sage, parsley and bread crumbs. Season with salt and pepper. Stir in egg.
3. Loosely stuff body cavity. Fasten neck skin to back of goose with skewers. Truss goose. Prick goose skin all over to allow fat to escape during roasting.
4. Place goose, breast-side up, on a roasting rack in a roasting pan. Insert a meat thermometer in center of inner thigh without touching bone, if desired.
5. Roast in preheated oven 45 to 60 minutes or until skin is well browned. Pour off fat from pan. Place a foil tent loosely over goose. Roast about 2 hours more or until thermometer registers 180F (80C) or until juices run clear when pierced between thigh and breast.
6. Place goose on a warmed serving dish; keep warm. To make gravy, spoon off all but 3 tablespoons fat from pan. Stir in flour, scraping up any browned bits. Cook 1 minute, stirring. Gradually stir in wine and stock. Cook, stirring, until thickened. Add lemon juice to taste, if desired.
7. Garnish goose with onions, carrots and parsley. Serve with peas cooked with crumbled cooked bacon and chopped onion, if desired. Makes 8 to 10 servings.

Top to bottom: Bûche de Noël, Peas à la française, Roast Goose

# New Year's Cake

GREECE

| | |
|---|---|
| 2-3/4 cups all-purpose flour | 2 cups sugar |
| 4 teaspoons baking powder | 4 eggs |
| 1 teaspoon grated nutmeg | Grated peel of 1 large orange |
| 1/2 teaspoon salt | 1 cup orange juice |
| 1 cup butter or margarine, room temperature | 1/3 cup sliced almonds |

*This cake is served at the stroke of midnight on New Year's Eve in Greece. This version is much smaller than the cakes prepared in Greece for New Year's Eve. The traditional cake always has a lucky coin baked in it, but ingredients may vary from family to family. If the lucky coin is in one of the first three pieces, everyone present is supposed to have a happy year. Cake that is not served to guests is to be given to the poor the next day.*

**1.** Preheat oven to 350F (175C). Grease a 13" x 9" baking pan. Line bottom and sides of pan with waxed paper; grease paper.
**2.** Sift flour, baking powder, nutmeg and salt into a medium bowl; set aside.
**3.** In a large bowl, beat butter or margarine and sugar until light and fluffy. Beat in eggs, 1 at a time, beating well after each addition. Beat in orange peel.
**4.** Add flour mixture to egg mixture alternately with orange juice; beat until blended. Wrap a coin in foil; add to batter, if desired. Pour batter into prepared pan; smooth top. Sprinkle with almonds.
**5.** Bake in preheated oven 55 to 60 minutes or until cake springs back when lightly pressed in center. Cool in pan on a wire rack 30 minutes. Carefully lift cake out of pan; cool completely on wire rack, nut-side up. Peel off lining paper. Makes 16 servings.

# Ao 'a' tea Roa

NEW ZEALAND

| | |
|---|---|
| 1-1/2 cups all-purpose flour | 2 teaspoons baking soda |
| 1-1/4 cups firmly packed light-brown sugar | 1-1/2 cups boiling water |
| 2 teaspoons grated lemon peel | 2 eggs, beaten |
| 1/2 teaspoon ground cinnamon | *Topping:* |
| 1 cup golden raisins | 1 (16-oz.) can apricot halves |
| 2 cups dark raisins | 1/2 teaspoon ground cinnamon |
| 1/4 cup chopped mixed candied fruit | 8 to 10 rectangular slices vanilla ice cream |
| 1/2 cup butter or margarine | 2 to 3 tablespoons brandy |

*The Maori name for this Christmas pudding, Ao 'a' tea Roa, describes the long white cloud always visible over the islands of New Zealand as you fly in. Roast turkey, traditionally served on Christmas Day, is followed by this dessert. This pudding which is light and airy is appropriate for New Zealand's warm sunny Christmas weather.*

**1.** Sift flour into a medium bowl. Stir in brown sugar, lemon peel and cinnamon until blended. Stir in raisins and mixed fruit. Cut butter or margarine into pieces; place on top of fruit mixture.
**2.** Dissolve baking soda in boiling water; pour over fruit mixture and butter or margarine. Stir until combined. Cover bowl with a clean towel; let stand overnight in a cool place.
**3.** Next day, grease a 2-1/2-quart heatproof bowl. Stir eggs into fruit mixture, stirring with a wooden spoon until blended. Pour mixture into greased bowl; smooth top. Grease a double thickness of waxed paper large enough to cover bowl. Cover bowl with greased waxed paper. Wrap with foil; tie with kitchen string.
**4.** Place bowl on a rack in a large deep saucepan. Pour in enough boiling water to come halfway up side of bowl. Cover and steam pudding over low heat 3 hours, adding more water as necessary to maintain water level.
**5.** Line an 11" x 4" loaf pan with foil; grease foil. Remove pudding from saucepan; uncover. Let stand 30 minutes. Spoon warm pudding into prepared loaf pan, packing pudding into bottom and sides of pan with back of a spoon. Cover and refrigerate until served.
**6.** To make topping, drain apricots, reserving 2 to 3 tablespoons syrup. In a blender or food processor fitted with a steel blade, process apricots and reserved syrup until pureed. Pour apricot puree into a bowl; stir in cinnamon. Refrigerate until served.
**7.** To serve, remove pudding from refrigerator; invert onto a long serving plate. Peel off foil. Arrange ice-cream slices on top of pudding; spoon apricot puree over ice cream. Warm brandy in a small saucepan; pour around pudding. Carefully ignite brandy; serve while flaming. Makes 8 to 10 servings.

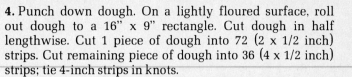

# Spanish Honey Fritters

SPAIN

| | |
|---|---|
| 1 teaspoon sugar | About 3 cups all-purpose |
| 1 (1/4-oz.) package active | flour, sifted |
| dry yeast (1 tablespoon) | Vegetable oil for deep |
| 1/4 cup warm milk | frying |
| (110F, 45C) | Honey |
| 1 teaspoon salt | About 1/3 cup chopped |
| 4 eggs, beaten | toasted almonds or |
| 3 tablespoons brandy | hazelnuts |

1. In a medium bowl, dissolve sugar and yeast in milk. Let stand 5 to 10 minutes or until foamy. Stir in salt, eggs and brandy until blended.
2. Stir in 2 cups flour or enough flour to make a soft dough. On a lightly floured surface, knead in enough remaining flour to make a stiff dough. Knead 8 to 10 minutes or until smooth and elastic.
3. Clean and grease bowl. Place dough in greased bowl, turning to coat all sides. Cover with a slightly damp towel. Let rise in a warm place, free from draft, until doubled in bulk.
4. Punch down dough. On a lightly floured surface, roll out dough to a 16" x 9" rectangle. Cut dough in half lengthwise. Cut 1 piece of dough into 72 (2 x 1/2 inch) strips. Cut remaining piece of dough into 36 (4 x 1/2 inch) strips; tie 4-inch strips in knots.
5. Heat oil in a deep-fat fryer to 375F (190C) or until a 1-inch bread cube turns golden brown in 50 seconds. Deep-fry knots and strips, a few at a time, 2 to 2-1/2 minutes or until golden brown, turning once. Remove with a slotted spoon; drain on paper towels. Repeat with remaining knots and strips.
6. Dip a wet pastry brush in honey; brush honey over fritters. Arrange on a serving plate; sprinkle with nuts. Serve warm or cold. Makes about 108.

Left to right: Ao 'a' tea Roa, Spanish Honey Fritters, New Year's Cake

# Index

---